What the heck
just happened?

A
MIRACLE!

"Their Chickens have
come home to roost!"

My Personal Half Century Battle Against the Democrat/Socialist Party

GENE NELSON ISOM

What the Heck Just Happened? A MIRACLE!
"Their Chickens Have Come Home to Roost!"
All Rights Reserved.
Copyright © 2019 Gene Nelson Isom
v2.0

The opinions expressed in this manuscript are solely the opinions of the author and do not represent the opinions or thoughts of the publisher. The author has represented and warranted full ownership and/or legal right to publish all the materials in this book.

This book may not be reproduced, transmitted, or stored in whole or in part by any means, including graphic, electronic, or mechanical without the express written consent of the publisher except in the case of brief quotations embodied in critical articles and reviews.

Huckleberry Heart Publishing

ISBN: 978-0-578-20867-1

Cover Photo © 2019 www.gettyimages.com. All rights reserved - used with permission.

PRINTED IN THE UNITED STATES OF AMERICA

OTHER BOOKS BY THE AUTHOR

Good Old Olive Branch, The Way it Was!

Huckleberry Heart, The Boys of Halloran Avenue

Just Another American Family

This is who I am! What are You?

In loving memory of the one that never doubted me and always provided encouragement for all my foolish endeavors; my beautiful and loving wife, Doris Ann Legg Isom

Table of Contents

Acknowledgements i
About this Book? iii
About this Book Cover! v
America, Why I Love her! vii
Prologue ix
Introduction xiii
My Prognostications xix
How do you destroy Greatness xxiii

PART ONE: Subjects for debate

Political Correctness! 3
Our Uneducated Youth! 4
The character difference between Democrats and Republicans! 7
The Electoral College and why? 9
Genital Neutral Bathrooms! What? 11
Affirmative Action! 14
Reparations! Really? For whom? 16

Some great quotes to think about! 19
Words of Wisdom 21

PART TWO

This is who I am! 25
Older letters to my email list 28
The Best of 2015 (From Ike's Desk) 35
The Best of 2016 (From Ike's Desk) 53
Epilogue 142

Acknowledgements

It is always difficult to give credit where due when acknowledging those individuals that you feel have contributed the most to the completion of your final work. Although my precious wife, Doris Ann, is no longer with me for the completion, she is none-the-less, responsible by her faith, patients and encouragement that she has provided over the years. I give much credit to our national news media and the Democrat Party for their unbridled dishonesty and corruption of their constitutionally given rights. Their extreme left wing biased and partisanship left me no choice except to counter with my political letters and emails, "From Ike's Desk," which is the primary basis for this book. I also must acknowledge the many readers that provided positive feedback that helped keep the drive alive during the trying days of the 2015-16 Presidential campaigning. Last, and probably the most important reason this book exists is because of Hillary Clinton may have been the most inapt candidate the Democrat Party could ever have nominated for President of the Untied State of America!

About this Book?

The title of this book was to be "Wake up America!" because I had been using that phase for about fifteen years at the ends of my many political emails and Posts. However, Eric Bolling beat me to it with his best seller by that title that hit the market in 2016. The phrase was first nationally used in a Poster by James Montgomery Flagg in 1917, the same individual that made the most famous poster first used during World War One and then again during the Second World War during the early 1940's. It was an Uncle Sam Poster pointing at you with a stern look with the caption of: "I want you for the U.S. Army" However, with that title gone, I had to come up with another working title and I chose "Well I told you so! Damn it!" In case Donald Trump lost. With his miraculous win over Hillary Clinton I had to change it again to one that more accurately describing the shock of a Donald Trump victory; "What the heck just happened! A MIRACLE!" had to be it with a subtitle "Their chickens have come home to Roost!" referring to the idiom first credited to Robert Southey in 1809 who wrote "Curses are like young chickens, they always come home to roost." If chickens are coming home to roost, someone is suffering the unpleasant consequences of their bad actions in the past. The curses and causes of the Democrat Socialist Party have rightly come back to bite them in their derriere with Trump's win over Hillary Clinton. The term regained popularity a few years ago when used by President Obama's mentor for twenty years, Reverend Jeremiah Wright.

This book will serve as the history of what just happened; covering the one year period of the 2016 Presidential Campaigning as I witnessed and wrote about on a continuing basis. Also I leave no doubt as to why I believe Donald Trump was the wrong choice as the Republican Nominee even though, and it hurts me to say this, he may turn out to be the only Republican Candidate that could have possibly beaten Hillary Clinton, but why? Why in America today it took a rabblerousing misfit for the office of President of the United States to defeat a candidate for the office of President that by all past standards could never have qualified as a candidate for Dog-Catcher in Podunk, Illinois? The answer to that question lies within the degradation of our educational system within our country over the past several decades and is discussed in more detail within this book. .

About this Book Cover!

I want the book cover to say it all with just a glance. By the U.S. Capital Building alone I want it to remind us all that the United States of America with its Liberating Constitution is the greatest country every devised by man. I want it to be so loud in color that it could not possibly be avoided to be instantly noticed on any book shelf that it may happen upon. It may not ever be purchased or read, but they should never be able to say they didn't notice it.

America, Why I Love her!

I must enter this vignette here because of its beautiful and profound description of our country. I first heard it many years ago when it was released and narrated by John Wayne and recorded on a large 78 RPM record that were being used at that time. From that moment on, any time I needed my patriotic fix, and that would happen often, I would play this record. In fact I've played it so often over the years that I now have it memorized and have on occasions been ask to recite it. The feeling of love and dedication for ones country is a warm and beautiful thing. Patriotism toward ones country is vital for the preservation of a stable social order. We can see what happens to a country right here in America when the word **PATRIOTISM** becomes Politically Incorrect. The reading of this vignette from the album, America Why I Love Her, gave me that feeling the first time I read it and I suppose it is because I have been there and done that, except visit Alaska that has caused its words to have a lasting impact upon my life.

WHY I LOVE HER

By
John Mitchum

America…You ask me why I love her? Well, give me time and I'll explain.
Have you seen a Kansas sunset or an Arizona rain?
Have you drifted on a bayou down Louisiana way?
Have you watched the cold fog drifting over San Francisco Bay?
Have you heard the bobwhite calling in the Carolina Pines
Or heard the bellow of a diesel at the Appalachia mines?
Does the call of the Niagara thrill you when you hear her waters roar?
Do you look with awe and wonder at her Massachusetts shore…
Where men, who braved a hard new world, first stepped on Plymouths Rock?
And do you think of those men when you stroll a New York City dock?
Have you seen a snowflake drifting in the Rockies…way up high?
Have you seen the sun come blazing down from a bright Nevada sky?
Do you hail to the Columbia as she rushes to the sea…
Or bowed your head at Gettysburg…at our struggles to be free?
Have you seen the mighty Tetons?…Have you watched an eagle soar?
Have you seen the Mississippi roll along Missouri's shore?
Have you felt a chill at Michigan, when on a winter's day,
Her waters rage along the shore in thunderous display?
Does the word "Aloha"…make you warm?
Do you stare in disbelief when the surf comes roaring in at Waimea reef?
From Alaska's cold to the Everglades…from the Rio Grande to Maine…
My heart cries out… my pulse runs fast at the might of her domain.
You ask me why I love her?… I've a millions reasons why.
My beautiful America…beneath God's wide, wide sky.

Prologue

Who I am or what I would become, started on September 5, 1929 in the small community of Roxana, Illinois. The early years of my life were spent during the Great Depression of the 1930s that rocked this nation beyond anything it had experienced before. The true unemployment rate was at times better than 25 percent. Men walked the alleyways looking into garbage cans for scraps of food and knocked on back doors begging for handouts. I remember the times my mother would fix a plate of whatever was left over from the evening meal and allow the beggar (ally bums we called them) to eat it on the back porch steps. Sometimes they would ask for a potato, carrot or other vegetable along with any meat that could be given, to be then taken to Hobo Junction and along with the gatherings of others, mix them into a large pot and prepared into what was referred to as Hobo Stew.

It was also during this period of great hardship and suffering that our nation received another severe blow with the spreading of the great polio epidemic. Literally hundreds of thousand throughout the country were struck down by this disease for which there was no defense. It was non-discriminating; it struck rich or poor, the great or humble, young and old alike with extreme debilitating effects. Many died and others were left with its crippling effects for the rest of their lives. It struck our family in 1934 when my sister Norma became ill and was diagnosed with Polio. She survived but was permanently crippled in both legs and has suffered with its effects to this day.

I remember little of my first home on 2nd Street in Roxana, because we moved from there when I was still only two years old. It was at 114, 4th Street in Roxana that the world around me began to come into focus. That house too is now gone; demolished a few years ago.

During the next thirteen years we lived at six different addresses in Roxana, South Roxana, Wood River, Glendale Gardens and East Alton. This takes me up to just short of my sixteenth Birthday when in 1945 I walked out of the Wood River High School never to returned. I was never a good student anyway and always felt that my time was being wasted while sitting in a class room; and sitting was about the extent of it because my mind was never there. I was lost in thought of the woods, creeks and ponds; catching dozens of catfish, or fighting with our soldiers overseas during WWII. I couldn't wait until I was old enough to join the military service. I even tried to forge my own birth certificate, but blotched it badly and later had to have it reissued. Playing football was my only school interest. So, understanding that time spent in the classroom was starting to severely interfere with my education, I left.

The 1930s and early 1940s were an exciting and adventurous time for young boys and ours was no exception. My life during this period can be read in two books that I wrote and was published during 2006 and 2008 titled "Huckleberry Heart, The Boys of Halloran Avenue." And "Good Old Olive Branch, The way it was."

I joined the Army at age seventeen 0n January 4, 1947 and took basic training in Ft. Knox, Kentucky. Before our basic training was complete there were rumors that we were going to be the first of President Truman's UMT, Universal Military Training (UMTEES) as the program was referred to. It was rumored that we would be spending one year at Ft. Knox training as universal soldiers. Our training was to include Armored, Artillery, Infantry and other specialties, then spend six years in the reserves to be called upon when needed. However, the program was cancelled, or never really got off the ground before our training cycle was complete, therefore we ending up as Regular Army, which is what I originally thought I was joining for. My Army career ended after seven years in January 1954. I returned home to Olive Branch, Illinois and Married my home town sweetheart, Doris Ann Legg on April 10, 1954.

In August 1954 the country was going through hard times and Jobs were scares. I worked as a Fuller Brush salesman for a time in Cairo, Illinois before being talked into joining the Air Force by the local Recruiter. I spent the next three years in my old Army specialty at Scott Air Force Base, Illinois. With promotions frozen in that career field I requested a transfer to aircraft mechanics and after tech school at Chennault Air force Base, Illinois and spent the next eleven years with Strategic Air Command with various jobs on B-52 Bombers; serving in Westover Air Force Base, Massachusetts; McCoy Air Force base, Orlando, Florida and Kinchloe Air Force Base, Sault Ste Marie, Michigan; Retiring in October 1967, with a total of twenty-one years military service.

Introduction

What the Heck just Happened?

Today is November 9, 2016 and the election for the next President of the United State has miraculously been won by Donald Trump; the most inapt person I ever expected to become a sitting President. His victory over Hillary Clinton, who from the very beginning had already received their coronation as the next President by political pundits, especially the left-wing media, which is made up of most of the news organizations within the united States. She was well ahead in the polling early in 2015 when polling first started and still ahead in the polls that were being published a few days before the election. The political pundits, especially the leftwing media, which was, and still is at this writing, the most corrupt in the history of our nation and was one of the fears our founding father stressed when debating our Constitution. They knew that unbiased but critical news outlets would be necessary to maintain the free will of the American citizen and provide the knowledge for the individual citizen to make honest and personal judgments about their political lives; they truly feared what our news outlets have become today. They knew our new Republic would never survive long with a corrupt and biased Press. It would be hard pressed to imagine what our country would look like today had it not been for the intervention of the Cable News and the Internet?

Without detailing my personal opinion of Donald Trump at this point, which I have adequately stressed within my many posts throughout the 2016 campaigning period, will try to explain here, in my humble opinion, of what the heck just happened in a broad sense. First, the Democrats were stuck with Hillary regardless of whether the more intelligent among them wanted her or not. After all, it was her turn, Bill had said so, therefore, there could never have been an honest attempt by the Democrat Party Apparatchik to even try to replace her with a more suitable candidate. She had been running for President for over twenty-four years; since the moment she became the First Lady and probably even before that. Her loss to Barack Obama during the Primaries of 2007 was an unexpected shock that took some time for her to get over, but that defeat in no why dampened that burning fever of becoming the first woman President of the United States of America. Her driving and unhealthy ambition for fame and lasting glory never diminished during the following eight years and her turn finally came and if it hadn't been for a sudden surge of hesitant Republicans and responsible thinking citizens at last knowing they had no other choice, turning out in large numbers in those states that really mattered the last two days before the election, she would be the President elect today instead of Donald Trump. I predicted earlier in the campaign that many reluctant Republicans that had originally stated that they could never vote for Trump would eventually come back because they really had no chose; and thank God I'm sure most did.

I must admit that her concession speech was something that I never expected from her. What was said; how much Blankety-Blank profanity went on behind closed doors we may never know, but you can be assured there were plenty. For those that have known the full history of Hillary Clinton, know it would have been out of character for her not to release at least a few of her favorite expletives because of Trump's victory over her. However, her concession speech was gracious and very professional; yes, and very surprising.

Having said that I have to admit it is really out of character for Hillary, so being the skeptic that I am, I ask myself, why would she act this way when by all previous evidence she should have pitch a real big public hissy. I honestly believe it may be because she is still under investigation and an indictment may yet come her way. This goody-goody performance may have been a feeble and last minute attempt to help soften the blow that's coming if she doesn't receive a pardon by President Obama before he leaves office. If that should happen, it would be so unfair to all those who have been severely punished and some still today doing time for the same crime or much less than she. If President Obama gives her a Pardon, Trump upon his talking the Oath of office should do likewise and Pardon all previous offenders for the same crime against the Untitled States of America that Hillary has committed.

On the other side we have Donald Trump, the most unlikely candidate the Republican Party could have possibly chosen for their nominee. I have said from the very beginning that Donald Trump was not really serious about becoming President when he first announced his candidacy, nor was his demeanor or personality suited to be President of the United States. In my opinion this started out as an ego trip. Trump's ego constantly hungers for adulation and praise. Somewhere along the way he noticed that the people were agreeing with everything he said and their numbers grew into a real force to be reckoned with. He finally came to the conclusion that he could possible become President of the most powerful nation on earth; just how much higher could an ultra ego go than that? Although he did not receive a majority of Republican Primary votes, he did receive all he needed to become the Republican Party nominee and eventually the President Elect of the United States of America.

Within his victory speech, in my opinion, he overly emphasized the need for unity going forward. He stressed the need to work with all parties on bringing our divided nation back together. At this writing, the day after his victory I have great concern about just how much give and take for the sake of unity there will be; and who will gave and who will take. I've never known the Democrat Party ever to willing accept anything less than one-hundred percent of the whole loaf. Their definition of compromise has always been to get the bigger share, if not all. History has proven me right on this and it has also proven that the Republican Party for the last decade or so has been willing to give most it their share away for the sake of compromising; that is why we are almost a solid Socialist Nation today.

During these last eight years of the Obama administration the Republican leadership totally failed their constituency as well as all our citizens. Obama new from the beginning that the Republican leadership would tread lightly because of the color of his skin, however, had he realized they would not tread upon him at all, what disaster he could have created upon the future of our Nation. There is no telling how much more damage Obama could have done to our social and economic lives as well as our prestige and degradation around the world.

My concern at this point, with basically the same Republican leadership still in place and now a Republican President, our future remains an uncertainty. Will they have the courage to correct the trends of the past decade? Will Trump compromise on those areas that will make the biggest impact directly upon the lives of the citizens? I believe his biggest compromise may be on the nominee for the Supreme Court. Hopefully his quest for unity will not be the nomination of a moderate for the Supreme Court. If that happens we can still kiss our Constitution goodbye. There has never been a moderate yet appointed by the Republicans that didn't at some time turn around and bite the American people in the ass. If on the other hand he destroys the pretext of unity and does the right thing and chooses a Constitutionalist, such as Ted Cruz, or one of the finalists on the list he has published, then we will know he is serious about turning this country around and - Making America Great Again!

Trump is a business man and has been involved in many business negotiations during his business lifetime. He knows a good negotiation is coming away with more than you gave away. Trump knows this but in the near future as President, he will not be negotiating for his own monetary gain, but will be negotiating for the future of our country and all our lives and he must come away with more than he gives in order to satisfy his Trumpets and fulfill his political promises.

Remember the Proverb, first used in 1832 by Senator Marcy "To the victor belong the spoils." It became the Democrat Parties Modus Operandi over the last century and they have practiced it with expertise at every opportunity they've had; the Republicans, not so. For the last couple of decades they have given the spoils away just for the sake of unity. Let's hope Trump's quest for unity does not go as far as his recent predecessors. His Trumpets will not understand that kind of compromising and negotiating. It would have been better for him to have spent more time on words that emphasize making America Great Again and less on all this unity crap, because it will not work; it will not placate, or dampen the determination of the left's quest for total destruction of Trump and his administration.

Of course all this is supposition on my part at this time because Trump only became the President elect yesterday and we know to try to predict the future can be a risky thing as you will see while reading my many posts during 2016. We'll have to wait another few months to really get a feel of just how Trump intends to govern.

My Prognostications

To prognosticate is a dangerous business, especially concerning politics. The fickle political winds can change dramatically at any given moment with surprising results that can prove you wrong. So to attempt to tell the outcome of a political nature can be an uncertainty. However, when it comes to what Trump will, or will not accomplish, I feel safe in also predicting that he will fall well short of accomplishing fifty present of what he has promised. He will no doubt make some changes in every area he has promised and that alone well be a tremendous improvement over the direction our country was headed under the past administration, or would have been under Hillary Clinton, but will not fully satisfy his Trumpets; they will however accept it by finding a million excusing of why he could not accomplish what he promised, because to do otherwise would cause them to admit they chose the wrong candidate and few would ever admit that they could have been wrong; it's the nature of the species.

In my previous book, "This is who I am! What are you?" starting on page 9, I wrote the following:

> "However, today is July 4, 2014 and I feel we have now arrived at a critical crossroad. We either continue to the left and undoubtedly toward total Serfdom far greater than our

forefathers suffered under King George; and yes, their British Lords were overbearing and at times brutal in controlling the colonies, and politically it was taxation without representation which eventually leads to the Declaration of Independence and the Revolution that freed us from British rule. However, their Tierney was nothing compared to the bleak and dark existence facing future Americans under the suppressive and dictatorial clutches of the progressive's form of Socialism and Liberalism. The two are firmly intertwined; do not fool yourself in believing they are not one in the same.

Just maybe the administration of President Obama and the Democrat Party has now brought us to the point of Critical Mass and has awakened the sleeping giant. At least I hope that the giant has been nudged a little. With the controlling and dictatorial efforts of Obamacare and the Obama administration; the citizen are starting to say enough. As this number increases over the period of the next two years, it could just be that spark to ignite the flame of a rebirth of a patriotic America, where once again the citizens can be proud of their government and their country. However, unless those citizens that have become tired and worn down and dropped out by the overwhelming force of the liberal Democrat Party and their dominions, combined with and impotency of the Republican Party do not return to the fight, it will never happen. It will take every responsible thinking American, every disillusioned Christian to once again return to the fight. It was only because of their dropping out of the electoral process in 2012 that President Obama was elected to a second term. This must not happen in 2014 or 2016. Together, the responsible citizens of the last hope for mankind can make the difference between Serfdom or Liberty, if they ban together and vote as one large conservative block. If America is to be saved, control of the

Senate must change in 2014. If not, the changes that will take place within the following two years may be irreversible by 2016."

Much of this has happened and we now have control of both houses of Congress and Just maybe Trump's miraculous win over Hillary Clinton is the Clarion Call that will awaken the sleeping masses. Just maybe Trump is the spark that will once again ignite the flames of patriotism and pride within the soul of America. Maybe shirts with American Flags on them can once again be worn by students within the schools of California? Maybe American Flags will once again be flown from the staffs within our institutions of higher learning? Just maybe the heart braking scenes of the American Flags being burned or stomped on will become a rarity; Just Maybe? That maybe will depend completely upon Trump's ability to negotiate our Nation's political and social future as well as he has his personal business ventures. By early 2018 Trump's ability to govern our nation will be known. We will know if he will survive the masses of evil that will be thrown against his every attempt at fulfilling his promises. His advisories will be relentless in their pursuits to destroy him and his administration. We will either have bounced back with evidence of a robust economy and a healthy social order on the way, or continue to stagger along with many failures and disappointments. It will all depend upon the government he chooses and then his ability to allow them to govern with little personal interference. Just maybe...?

How do you destroy Greatness

By being Barack Hussein Obama

I wrote the following several years ago and I now have been proven right!

Today, Barrack Hussein Obama has not disappointed me. My predictions of his Presidency eight years ago when he was elected President has come to pass. I predicted he would go down in history rated at the bottom of the worst American Presidents, particularly by those that have not drink of the liberal/socialist Kool-Aid. I predicted Obama, who had spent his formative years in an environment of hate for America and our way of life could never govern as his oath of office mandates. The outcome of his Presidency could have ended no other way except a disaster for the citizens. Much of the success of his accomplishments can be directly contributed to the capitulation of responsibility by the leadership of the Republican Party for the past eight years; and I might add, most are still in charge.

"It boggles the mind to consider what greatness President Obama could have achieved had he been a true and honest American citizen? Had his goal been to unite instead of divide; improve upon on our almost perfect healthcare system instead of destroying it; correcting the corruption within our departments of government instead of encouraging it; strove to improve our image with our allies and other nations of the world instead of destroying their trust; secure our borders instead of opening them; reduced taxes to small businesses and encouraged the entrepreneurial spirit to increase jobs; worked to reduce welfare dependency instead of working overtime to increase it; honored his oath of office and worked to uphold our Constitution instead of disrespecting it; his mistakes are endless. Future generations would have bestowed upon him reverence far greater than they now bestow upon another great black American, Martin Luther King, who would then most likely become just another also mentioned, during Black History Month.

That greatness will never happen now because it was squandered by our country's first elected black President who turned out to be anti-American in almost every way imaginably. Could he strut and preen at pomp and ceremony, oh yes, at that he was the best. And yes, I'm sure there will be future statues and monuments scattered here and there throughout our nation, and yes by his own choice, they will receive their rightly due status; the depository for Pigeon droppings.

Have I just disrespected the office of the President of the United States of America? No, that title belongs to no other than Barrack Hussein Obama!"

PART ONE

Subjects for debate

Political Correctness!

How do you explain political correctness? To accept political correctness you must be willing to accept an untruth. You must also be willing to give up one of the major tenets of our Constitution, your freedom of speech. The Political Correct Doctrine dictates that you must always be on guard to not speak of things as they really are. The Truth will not set you free in the politically correct world that we live in today; it will only put you in the unemployment line. It is said that we as a country have the largest prison population in the world, but can the cause be publically and accurately stated by prominently positioned individuals and still keep their jobs; not likely? Many of the social evils that have befallen the United States citizens today can be directly attributed to our acceptance and adherence to the Politically Correctness Doctrine.

The fear of the consequences for speaking the truth within our society today has become so perverse that the truth in many cases is almost always avoided unconsciously. We as a society have accepted the fact that we must never allow the truth to slip from our lips. No! No! The truth in today's America will not set you free.

Our Uneducated Youth!

If we want to understand our youth today, we must start with the source of their education, or the lack of concern for that education by a majority of parents throughout our country and probably a governmentally controlled education purposely directed toward the destruction or belief in the virtues of our Democratic Republic as debated during the Constitutional Convention of 1787. The Federal Department of Education should never have existed under our Federalist system of government. Money drained from the States to feed a massive and corrupt Federal bureaucracy that has become our Department of Education should have remained in the States to spend on their educational system as they see fit; that's called Federalism.

The Department of Education was first established in 1867 as a department, but was reduced to an Office one year later. It became a Cabinet Level Department in 1979 with a budget of 12 billion. Today it has grown into a massive bureaucracy starting with the Secretary, The Deputy Secretary and the Under Secretary with over 28 separate departments below them at a cost of 68 Billion and 4,400 employees. These Billions of dollars would have remained in the states had Ronald Reagan eliminated this department as he suggested when running for President.

Dictates from the Department of Education have been detrimental to the advancement of a basic education of our youth, but have successfully educated them in the social graces of Political Correctness. To give the readers a better understanding of exactly why we still have such an un-American Cabinet position still within our government after Ronald Reagan was so determined to abolish it after he became President you may want to read the letter dated, June 29, 2012 written by Sam Blumenfeld. It was evident that forces within his own administration were working with the progressives to increase control of the minds of our youth and they are still part of the Deep State, the socialist, buried deep within our bureaucracy that controls our government even today.

There was a Pew Poll released on February 15, 2017 that has some very interesting statistics that probably prove the Progressive Government Education System has had some very profound effects on our youth over the preceding years. The age group, 18-29 have become more tolerant of Muslims, atheist, and homosexual life styles and less tolerant of Religion. To be tolerant of other life styles may show compassion and understanding, but at the same time may allow a tendency of lowering the safeguards for maintaining a social structure that has provided the highest standards for social stability; also the most personal Liberty that the individual has ever experienced in the history of mankind.

Another proof that our young people are becoming indoctrinated with left leaning tendencies may be because of their inability to record radical leftwing indoctrination by their socialist professors. The schools and these professors want the right to indoctrinate these soft brains of mush without interference from outside. They know that their lies and deception will be exposed and countered by the truth from adult influences if revealed. Their indoctrination can only continue as long as it remains within the classroom. If a professor is honestly teaching a required subject toward a degree why wouldn't they want the students to record it; isn't that the whole reason for the class? Evidently those professors have other motives aside teaching just the subject that the students signed up for.

Our schools must not be allowed to curtail the first amendment rights of their students. The Department of Education must be abolished and those billions of dollars being spent for the purpose of "*Dumbing Down America*" must be return to the state level to be used for basic education and not *Social Engineering*.

The character difference between Democrats and Republicans!

I could fill a major size book on this subject alone because of the differences in character between the two parties, but what is character? According to my dictionary it is: A distinctive trait, quality, attribute, a pattern of behavior found in a group, moral behavior, etc., etc.

As I became more involved in current events and politics during the past fifty years, the differences in the character of the two major parties became more evident. In the beginning of my awareness I believe the two parties displayed much of the same traits of character but basically believed, and tried to convince the people that they could serve them better than the opposing party, and to a certain level this was correct, except the trends and actions of the Democrat Party, although very subtle, was always directed toward the eventual state of socialism even though the rank and file members were totally unaware of it. The Republican Party on the other hand was trying to convince the citizens that their political philosophy was that of the founders and adherence to the Constitution. The democrat socialist philosophy was more appealing to the majority of the people because of all the goodies they promised and in an era of social upheaval of the 1920-30s they were hard to refuse and more and more citizens were drawn into the

Democrat Party.

By the 1960s the fight for the soul of America became more intense and obvious of exactly what each party really stood for by their published political platforms. I have written about these differences over the years, but once again must point them out here in this book.

The Republican Party believes in the Second Amendment as intended by our founding fathers. The Democrat Party does not. The Republican Party believes in Federalism; more control by the states and less control by the federal government. The Democrat Party believes in a larger, more intrusive government dictating events in the everyday lives of the citizens; for their own good of course. The Republican Party believes we as a sovereign nation have the right to control our borders and uphold our immigration laws. The Democrat Party believes in open borders for the sole purpose of increasing their voter rolls. The list of differences between the characters of the two parties is endless.

The real danger to our country lies within the direction the Democrat Party wants to take us and the ability of the Republican Party to stop their drive toward dragging our society farther toward a socialist state.

The Electoral College and why?

If there ever was a more perfect argument why our founding father established the Electoral College rather than electing our President by the Popular Vote, you have just witnessed it by the outcome of the recent Presidential Election. To really appreciate the great minds of our wise founders of that time, you must read the debates that took place in the hot summer months of July and August of 1787 in Philadelphia, during their Constitutional Convention.

The question of how and who would elect the President was debated long and hard and was dropped and revisited on several occasions, but eventually decided to have electors chosen by state legislators to choose the executive, as he was referred to at that time. Their reasoning at that time was the electors would be better informed than the general populace and would be a temporary body; therefore the executive could neither come under its influence nor seek its favor.

How the states would choose their electors and how many per state was also debated long and hard. Smaller states realized that the larger states would always elect the Executive if a fair distribution of electors was not settled upon. There wisdom is so obviously evident with the past election. Had The Electoral College system not been settled upon and our President chosen by popular vote, California alone would have elected Hillary Clinton and the rest of the states would have little input into who our President should be. When one extremely large state has become so radically separated politically and philosophically from the rest of the nation as we see California today, I now know why the wisdom of our founders never fails to amaze me.

I highly recommend the Book "The Constitutional Convention, A Narrative History" from the notes of James Madison.

Genital Neutral Bathrooms! What?

How far out into La-La Land can we get? Is there really no end to this social engineering of stupidity that is driving the rational minds of our citizens crazy? Must responsible news outlets continue to publish this insanity and call it NEWS just for the sake of making money and being considered fair and balanced by elements of our society that will never under any circumstances consider them being fair and balanced.

How many centuries have the Male and Female sign worked just fine to designate what public bathroom we were supposed to be using. The symbols designating the correct bathroom to use told you that if you were born with male genitals, you used the one marked with the symbol for male. On the other hand if you were born with Female genitals you used the one marked with the symbol of the Female.

Now after hundreds of years, at least since the inception of public bathrooms, it would appear that there wouldn't be anyone left on earth that doesn't understand which bathroom they should be using and of course understand the two bodily functions that they were constructed to serve. We now find that those individuals that feel they were born in the wrong body think these public bathrooms must serve a different function, and what could that possible be other than the two alimentary functions that bathrooms were built to accommodate?

Now please give this some serious thought. Have you ever been in a public bathroom that was built to provide for more than one occupant that did not provide privacy if you so desired. Larger male bathrooms are all equipped with stalls and urinals at your choosing. Female bathrooms all have stalls far privacy. Smaller one room bathrooms, both Male and female have locks and you may use either one at your discretion. So the question remains who is discriminating against whom because of their sexuality when it comes to which bathroom they have a right to use?

By what device or means of identity is to be used as proof to designate the right to choose a bathroom contrary to the genitals you were born with? Must transgender people carry and present proof that they have been designated by responsible medical authority to be different than the obvious, before using bathrooms contrary to their genitals? That wouldn't be very practical, would it, and who is going to man the doors?

Of course when it comes to the showers for those who feel they are transgender while they are still young and involved with athletics; may be emotionally uncomfortable showering with those they consider the opposite sex even if no one else knew the difference. Of course I'm sure older sexually mature transgender may have found it rather exciting to be in the shower with others of the same genitals; and please don't argue with this one!

The tremendous effort to accommodate the few at the expense of the many is just another way that social engineering by the radical left is slowly destroying our country and the supposedly responsible leadership is accommodating it. The expense and effort of accommodating the physically handicapped individuals within our society to function with minimum effort on a daily basis was the right thing to do because of the obvious, but bathrooms simply because of one's perception of being of a different sex than their genitals indicate? Get real? The possibility of exposing young people to perversion is a real possibility and fear of most parents with young children when using transgender bathrooms, or any bathrooms unattended. Crimes of sexual perversion will, especially against the young, increase in direct proportion to the increase of these deviant sexual policies.

Affirmative Action!

Does anyone remember the Affirmative Action Programs anymore? What happened to the drive to create fairness in employment and non-discrimination in education that was the rave of the liberal movement from 1962 on through the 1980s? Yes, I know many are still in place and still being practiced unconstitutionally.

President Kennedy in 1961 was the first to redress discrimination by introducing what was termed as "affirmative action" to counter discrimination in employment and education in spite of civil rights laws guaranteed by the constitution.

In 1964 President Johnson signed the 1964 Civil Rights Act into law that in my estimation actually outlawed preferential treatment as practiced within Affirmative Actions and sanctioned by the Supreme Court. The Supreme Court ruled that it was legal to discriminate against one group of citizens because of their color in preference for another because of a different color based on past discrimination policies. This ruling created what I consider the first major fracture, or rip, in our umbrella of equal protection guaranteed by our constitution as debated and affirmed.

I remember well in the 1980s when Affirmative Action practices were forced upon almost all major employers. The company that I was working for at the time actually forced employees to accept Affirmative Action by having the clause of adhering to Affirmative Action policy written into their annual evaluations forms of management personnel; failure to sign such an agreement would likely have had a major effect upon any consideration for future promotions within the company. I knew that Affirmative Action was discriminatory and argued heavily against it among my peers at the time, but signed the agreement anyway and have regretted it ever since. Going against what I knew to be right haunts me to this day.

Reparations! Really? For whom?

From time to time the call for reparations by certain black groups keeps popping up in the forefront of the daily news. Time and time again we have had to deal with this question as if it actually has legitimacy. In reality these black groups calling for reparations of past discrimination because of their ancestral plight of slavery is ridiculous and nothing more than an attempt to coerce our government into disbursing more of the taxpayer's hard earned money into their greedy hands.

To attempt to coerce money because of ancestral wrongs should never be condoned by today's standards of behavior against the contemporaneity of hundreds of years past. To better understand why their quest is not only foolish, but looking at today's plight of blacks in the United States of America would appear that they may have it absolutely backwards; who honestly owes whom?

We know that slavery existed from the beginning of recorded time the world over and obviously thousands of years before that. There is not a nation, region or society that didn't practice slavery as an accepted and normal condition of social conduct at sometime in their historical past. Now stop and think! After thousands of years of slavery, in less than two hundred years the practice has been almost eradicated around the world. In the few places where it may still exist to a point, it is frowned on seriously. You don't have to ask yourself why; you know because of some great wisdom demonstrated within the minds of our founding fathers and particularly the first sentence of the second paragraph of our Declaration of Independence which declares: "We hold these truths to be self-evident, that all men are created equal, that they are endowed by their Creator with certain unalienable rights, that among these are Life, Liberty and the pursuit of Happiness." No, that clause did not immediately set slaves free in the United States, or around the world, but it along with the abolitionist movement within this country was the catalyst that eventually ended slavery as an accepted condition of social life the world over.

What I'm about to say in this paragraph requires that I must tread lightly because of our current social blight of Political Correctness that prevails prominently within our society today. First, blacks living within our society today are owed nothing, unless they are over one-hundred-fifty-three years old. Those living in 1863 were on their way to live as free men the day that President Abraham Lincoln signed into law the Emancipation Proclamation. It was a struggle to overcome the many years of the Jim Crow era perpetuated by the Democrat Party and the southern states, but today they are here and have every opportunity as any citizens of this great nation. They can strive to achieve whatever they want; just as far as their talents and ambition will take them. Any handicaps in their way are of nature or of their own making and not of the privileged whites. There are millions of blacks, many extremely wealthy that prove they too can be whatever they choose to be. Does racism still exist today? Of course, and will continue to exist in many; blacks as well as white, but that cannot be used as reasons for blacks not to succeed in today's social environment.

If the ancestors of blacks living in America today had not been brought to this country as slaves, the majority of today's blacks would still be living in the dark bowels of Africa herding skinny cows and never knowing the liberated life that is available to them. I'm not really allowed to try to empathize with blacks in today's society because of my white privilege and political correctness, but if I could I think I would be down on my knees thinking God that I was born in America where our wise founding fathers, whose statues today are in danger of being destroyed, laid the groundwork for my freedom. For me, that would be all the Reparations I would need.

Now have I been insensitive to the black plight of today and Politically Incorrect, or have I just stated the truth and the obvious that could possibly get me fired, if I had a job?

Some great quotes to think about!

(Plus my comments)

Thomas Jefferson - "If a nation expects to be ignorant and free, in a state of civilization, it expects what never was and never will be." (He forecast our current Department of Education!)

Ronald Reagan - "The most terrifying words in the English language are: I'm from the government and I'm here to help you." (He is more right today than the day he wrote this.)

Ronald Reagan - "The trouble with our liberal friends is not that they're ignorant: It's just that they know so much that isn't so." (And with the debt debate they continue to prove it!)

Ronald Reagan - "Government is like a baby: An alimentary canal with a big appetite at one end and no sense of responsibility at the other." (All together now: OBAMA!!!)

Ronald Reagan - "Politics is a bad profession. If you succeed there are many rewards, if you disgrace yourself you can always write a book." (And there are many best sellers to be had!)

Thomas Jefferson - "when the people fear their government that is Tyranny. When the government fear the people that is liberty." (Let's go to the polls and scare the hell out of Democrats and liberate ourselves!)

Unknown - "How long will it be before you admit that voting for Obama was a mistake?" (For the Liberal left and the politically ignorant, Never!)

Benjamin Franklin - "Democracy is like two wolves and a lamb voting on what to have for lunch. Liberty is a well armed lamb contesting the vote." (And Obama is trying his best to disarm our lamb!)

Unknown - "The greatest trick the devil ever pulled was convincing the world that he didn't exist." (And many of our Christians today have fallen for it.)

Gene Nelson Isom - "Liberalism as a means of governing is pure economic, social and political evil. Conservatism is sanity with a large dose of benevolence."

Gene Nelson Isom – "Time has no shelf life. Use it or lose it, but can be forever captured in a photograph."

Gene Nelson Isom – "Destroying a photograph is destroying a moment in time captured, never to return."

Gene Nelson Isom – "Ask not what you can do for me, ask what you can do for my country. Take care of my country and my country will take care of me."

Gene Nelson Isom – "The pleasure of momentary satisfaction from infidelity is short lived, but the joy of knowing fidelity to your partner will last a lifetime."

Gene Nelson Isom – "Don't tell me what's wrong with the other candidate, tell me what's right with you."

Words of Wisdom

(And mine)

Aesop – "We hang the petty thieves and appoint the great ones to public office." (Never argue with Aesop)

Plato – "Those who are too smart to engage in politics are punished by being governed by those who are dumber" (And he has been proven right ever since)

Khrushchev – "Politicians are the same all over. They promise to build a bridge even where there is no River" (And Massachusetts set out to prove it)

Clarence Darrow – "When I was a boy I was told that anyone could become President; I'm beginning to believe it." (And Clarence, now you can!)

Author Unknown – "Why pay money to have your family tree traced: go in politics and your opponents will do it for you." (You do want the truth don't you?)

Jay Keno – "If God wanted us to vote, he would have given us candidates." (A lesson for the Republicans)

John Quinton – "Politicians are people who, when they see light at the end of the tunnel, go out and buy more tunnels." (What Light? What Tunnel?)

Ascar Ameringer – "Politics is the gentle art of getting votes from the poor and campaign funds from the rich, by promising to protect each from the other." (And we fall for it)

Addle Stevenson – "I offer my opponents a bargain: if they stop telling lies about me, I will stop telling the truth about them." (Newt should have used this)

Doug Larso – "Instead of giving politicians keys to the city, it would be better to change the locks." (No difference, they'll rob it either way)

PART TWO

This is who I am!

I have always been an Idealist as well as a believer in Constitutional textualism. I've always believed that both were inherently acquired before I exited the womb. The patriotism and belief in the Constitution as debated and written wasn't taught or environmentally achieved; I believe it was planted in my genes the moment of conception, because from my earliest awareness, both ideals have been with me and changed only in a sense of a better understanding of both.

Only toward my middle to later years have I been able to fully understand both even though I still have problems trying to express them to affect the results I strive for. However, neither belief has been influenced over time by social upheaval created by poor legislation or the courts; they were only hardened by them into a more crystal clear understanding of how the lives of free men should be lived.

Much of my lack of ability to express intelligently my thoughts concerning my beliefs may very well be the result of little formal education due to my adventurist wanderlust as a teenager. Bored beyond all relevance of what was happening within the walls of academia, left me no choice but to seek education elsewhere. By the time my middle teenage years were over, I had experienced most of life's good and bad; from death to cruelty; love to hate; hot to cold; loneliness to companionship, and just about every other emotion that a human will endure by the time they reach middle age. By the time I joined the Army at the age of seventeen, I was already a man in every sense of the word.

As I have outlined in my previous book, "This is who I am! What are you?" This book is compiled of the many posts "From Ike's Desk." There was much to write about during the campaigning of 2015-16, and much of what I wrote was never published, but I've included some of those posts and comments here in this book.

Note: The only degree I hold is a Doctorate of "SOHK" School of Hard Knocks. I walked out of High School not yet sixteen because of pure boredom and total disinterest and decided to leave and become educated, and what an education it turned out to be.

In the Fall of 1945 while sitting in an English class at the Wood River, Illinois High School, we were given an assignment to make a book report and hand it in by a certain date by our English teacher; name forgotten, along with every other teacher I had throughout my time spent in the classroom, with the exception of Miss. Harriet Stevenson, who took a personal interest in me and who I've always credited with my ability to graduate the eighth grade. Knowing this book assignment would take a lot of homework, which I had an extreme aversion to and lived by the belief that home and school were two different places and the twain should never meet, I decided enough is enough and at the end of the class, I walked to my hallway locker, threw my books in, locked it and walked out the back door, never to return. I've often wondered what I had left in my looker and how long was it before the Janitor cut the lock off and who cleaned it out? Too my knowledge, my family was never contacted by the school and never received any of my personal belongings that may have been left in the locker.

That day in 1945 was the first day of an education that could never have been acquired in any academic setting. My love of reading the classic adventurous novels of that time was the basis of my ability to continue to educating myself in most current affairs by my insatiable need to read. I've said on more than one occasion that my hunger to read something was as strong at times as my hunger for food. There would be many occasions in many different settings that I would search the area for any newspaper or magazine to satisfy that hunger. To this day I give credit for my insatiable need to read for whatever knowledge I have gained outside any academic setting.

Older letters to my email list

(Some letters are replies to questions asked)

Are the American people stupid?

(Jonathan Gruber and our political leaders think we are!)

And so do I. Yes, collectively we are a stupid people. Perhaps I could substitute a more acceptable word in place of stupid; however, it doesn't change the destructive effects our actions have had upon our political, social and economic life style for the past seventy years.

Yes! We are stupid for electing the same individuals decade after decade with no more thought than we would in picking out the best nonstick frying pan. We give more thought and research into buying the latest cell phone or electronic gadget than we do in voting for an individual with the power to make laws and pick judges that can have devastating results upon our social and economic wellbeing in so many ways.

We are stupid to think that either party leadership has the answer or the knowledge to correct the illegal immigration problem that they themselves have created through intent and incompetence, and we for not holding them responsible. With each reelection we have given them license to continue their destruction of our society as our founding fathers had intended it.

We are stupid for giving the government the right to take our schools away from local control and turning an education system that was once the best in the world only a couple of decades ago, to below the top twenty nations today.

Just because we have proven our stupidity in so many ways in the past, doesn't mean we have to remain that way. "Stupid is as Stupid does;" so let's stop being stupid.

Basically on November 4, 2014 we have done all we can to start the healing with the Republicans taking back the Senate and giving the Democrats a good political shellacking nationally. Just maybe there is one more miracle awaiting us in January. Just maybe there is enough strong willed and Constitutional loving Republican Senators and Congressmen with the courage to take the leadership away from Boehner and McConnell; that would indeed be the start of turning our nation back toward one that all Americans could be proud of and then just maybe we no longer would be thinking of ourselves as being stupid.

Gene N Isom

I don't argue politics?

Gene N Isom

February 23, 2014

How many times have you heard someone say, "I don't argue Politics or Religion!" Is it said because they feel so uninformed of either that they refrain because they're afraid they'll make an ass out of themselves? Or, is it because they know their beliefs are different from their friends, and they don't want to offend? I believe one or the other, or maybe both are correct for many.

I have to ask, what other two philosophies control our everyday existence more than Politics and Religion? Our lives are controlled daily because of politics; good and bad. Our daily activity, our conduct, in many ways is controlled by our religious beliefs. So why would the two most life controlling subjects be taboo for so many? I guess maybe because there never appears to be a winner even though it's a fact that there is a right and a wrong and when a wrong is spoken, whether verbally or in print, we must not remain silent.

No matter how free and vocal I am with my political views, I have found myself in the past discriminating when I forward political emails, but never religious. However, for the last twenty years I've become a staunch supporter and defender of liberty and have fought against every encroachment upon it from whatever source it may appear. I no longer will stay silent and hold back from defending it at every opportunity.

I believe our Constitution is the most perfect document ever devised by man for the preservation of Liberty for all mankind the world over. All defenders of our constitution must speak out in every instant they read or hear attacks upon it by the left. I will no longer stand silent while in a group and hear attacks being made upon conservatism or the Constitution. I will instantly counter with, I hope, an articulate and respectful, but honest opinion of why the attack was incorrect.

I know who I am and I know what I believe and will no longer remain among the Silent Majority that has been most responsible for the removal of Christianity from the public scene, or, the advance of socialistic trends within our society. I beg all freedom loving people to try to live by my axiom, "First, to thyself be true," and get over the stage fright or whatever is holding you back and speak out loud and strong and defend our Liberty and our Constitution…

My motto: Ask not what you can do for me; ask what you can do for my country; if you take care of my country, my country will take care of me!

Letter untitled or dated:

Anyone who has read the Koran knows the writer was correct and the questions ask were right on the mark. I've read it and it's a helter-skelter mishmash of revelations by the prophet Mohammed that our God would ever dictate; however the Devil probably would. It is almost impossible to understand.

One of the first observations that I have made during the past twenty years is the so-called moderate Muslim (there doesn't appear to be any) should be madder than hell at the radicals that have been stirring up all this resentment against their nation of Islam. If you stop to think about it they were accomplishing their caliphate slowly, but effectively by immigration. Given another fifty years and they would have their world wide caliphate without major resistance. Now however, the so-called radical terrorist perhaps has awakened a sleeping giant. Now their quest for world domination may be set back a few decades, but unless free and democratic nations of the world wake up, the inevitable will still happen. Without a declaration of war against the radical Islamic religion the world is about to return to the dark ages – but what do I know?

Ike

Letter untitled or dated:

Yes, we can celebrate the accomplishments of a capitalist system, but those accomplishments you speak of cannot be credited to any policy of Obama or his administration. They are due to the resilience of Capitalism – Not Obama!

I suppose most of those that have been opting for an increase in the minimum wage also should be happy this morning. The laws raising the minimum wage in 19 states just increased as of January 1st; another great accomplishment of the Left. The minimum wage has been raised six times since 1933 – Why? It was first raised to .25 cents; then in 1968 to $1.60; then in 1981 to $3.35; then in 1997 to $5.15; then in 2009 to $7.25 and it's going up again by the Feds. Again, WHY?

Here are some stats to think about:

In its study, UCSD researchers found that after minimum-wage increases, the national employment-to-population ratio decreased by 0.7 percent points between December 2006 and December 2012.

Increase in fast food prices to offset wag increase:

Big Mac Meal	$5.69 to $7.82
Steak Burrito Bowl	$6.65 to $9.14
3 Crunchy Taco Combos	$4.59 to $6.31
Whopper Meal	$6.15 to $8.46
Subway's Turkey Foot-long	$6.50 to $8.49

Well at least the hamburger slinger can afford it; they have just been given the means to pay for it. We know that it will not be just fast food prices that will be increased; the cost of everything chasing the money supply. This pretty well balances out for everyone except the poor and elderly on a very small fixed income. Their S.S. cost of living increase never really matches the cost of living increase or price increases. They're always just another step behind and the ones that suffer the most and create the need for the government to spend more for their welfare. Where does it end?

This spiral will continue as long as there are Left Wing Do-Gooders and governments continually mechanically manipulating price and wages. It's like a dog chasing his own tail. Supply and demand of prices and wages must seek its own level as certain as the physical nature of water.

I've seen firsthand what the effects of extorted wages can do compared against supply and demand wages. Union mechanics earned $19.00 per hr before a bankruptcy; partially due to high wages, went in search of $10.00 per hr. jobs after the bankruptcy and glad to get them.

I'm not an economist and know only what I've studied from some of the greatest economist this country has produced. I am convinced I'm right about this and the evil of Obama and Socialist Liberals and will continue to try to shine the light of truth on all their economic and socially destructive policies whenever I can. Gene

Letter Written Nov 27, 2014:

I wrote many years ago that Donkey Dung still stinks as does the increasing stench from the Democrat Party that it represents. Someone wrote back "Elephant S—t stinks worse!" My answer was "It takes a dumb dedicated Democrat to be a true connoisseur of animal crap; you had to have stuck your nose in both to know the difference."

It would be wonderful if we could rid this country of the stench of the social and political decay created by both parties over the years, but unfortunately we only have the two choices. One is to continue down the road to serfdom, and we know that is the only direction the Democrat Party will take us, or try to turn back that tide towards individual independence and freedom, that at least is the promise of the Republican Party, but I have my doubts with the current Republican leadership.

If our country is to be saved as the intent of the founders who created the most perfect covenant that free men should live by, then we have to vote Republican this November 4th. It is the only choice a true American has. We have to vote for the preservation of a social and political structure that will provide the most benefit for freedom and independence to our future generations regardless of any personal goodies we may lose. The future of our country is in the balance.

Hold your nose if you must, but by all means go vote this November 4th, and vote a straight Republican ballot! It's the only *Right* chose mature and responsible American voters have.

If you agree, pass it on, if you don't, tell me why. Gene N Isom

The Best of 2015
(From Ike's Desk)

FROM IKE'S DESK

April 15, – Here it comes again! **February 26, 2015**

I sometimes think that we Americans are the most stupid people in the world. Year after year we go through this ridicules ritual of dishonestly paying our taxes; at least a large part of our society are dishonest according to the IRS; those that have their taxes removed by payroll deduction end up contributing at least 99 percent of their taxes due. The rest of us cheat the government out of estimates running from 385 billion to 600 billion annually. Why there is this large a gap in the estimates is because the government doesn't have the foggiest idea of how much money is out there that could possibly be collected under a different tax system?

Not only has our Internal Revenue System become inexcusably inefficient, but it has also become a department of government that is a corrupt political tool of the Democrat Party and consequently proven to be an enemy of many segments of our society.

It is being reported that they cannot handle but 47 percent of the calls that come in to their offices. They have gone rouge; departed from the confines of a legal and honest department of our government and as long as we have this same Tax system and the same government leadership in place, there will be no justice in sight for many of our citizens until the citizen rise up and demand change; real change.

If the loses in billions annually is anywhere near accurate, what would be the estimate in trillions uncollected since this inefficient system was devised in the 1950s? It staggers the mind. Of course we had a different society when the Sixteenth Amendment was passed in 1913. Tax payers back then bragged about the amount of taxes they contributed to our government. They were proud of it; they were patriots. Today if there is any bragging at all, it would be those who tell us how much taxes they cheated the government out of; of course they don't call it cheating, they justify it as the right thing to do, because of the wasteful spending of the government.

Who is not paying their *Fare share* (I hate that term because of its subjectivity) you may ask; just about all of us to some degree, but mostly the criminal element and to some degree those that are self employed? But they, or none us, would be law breakers under a different system that collects every dollar that is taxable; and the best part is that no Internal Revenue System would be needed; that alone would eliminate 95,000 to 110,000 unnecessary employees that the tax payer would no longer have to support. Of course we would feel some sympathy for them because they'll have to go to work in the real world making half to one-third less than the government pays.

Folks, this is no pipe-dream! This is reality! The only reason we are still under this archaic and inefficient tax system is because of the leadership we have been electing to congress for the past fifty years; it is not in their best interest to change it. The democrats love it because of its socially progressive nature and Republicans love it because they, as well as the Democrats, buy votes by allocating tax credits to various segments of our society.

With a different system in place we could recapture many of those billions mentioned earlier by collecting taxes on money when it is being spent. No drug dealer or criminal organizations could escape paying *Their Fare Share* when they spend their ill gotten dollars. No self employed individual or business would need to consider ways to avoid taxes; they too would pay taxes on their income as it is spent and save hundreds of millions annually in tax preparation. Corporations would not feel the need to hide income in foreign banks; those dollars would come back to our shores. We as individuals would be in control of the amount of taxes we pay by our selection of what and how we buy and every family would get a monthly check from the government based on the cost of living index.

The ideal system of the several being proposed would be the FairTax System, because it is the only one that eliminates the IRS. The others would be better than what we have, except the corrupt IRS would need to remain in place although there could be a great reduction in the numbers of employees needed.

Every American should start giving serious thought to this as they struggle with their tax problems between now and April 15. Go to FairTax.org and check it out for yourself. There is not a question that cannot be answered. There are two books that have been published covering the FairTax system. The first titled "The FairTax Book" and the second "FairTax The truth" that answers all questions of opposition to the FairTax. Regardless of what system we change to, it's got to be better than this corrupt, wasteful and senseless system we're now using.

Gene N Isom

FROM IKE'S DESK

Lawlessness in Ferguson, Missouri!   March 12, 2015

President Obama and his Attorney General, Erick Holder are directly responsible for what is happening now in Ferguson, Missouri and around the country. Their partisanship and lack of responsible leadership, has created what we are witnessing today. Of course they had much help from other black leaders whose main goal is to create chaos for their own personal aggrandizement; does the name Al Sharpton come to mind? They are knowingly and are purposely manipulating a large segment of our society that are basically socially illiterate due to a lack of civic education in what is now referred to as government indoctrination; Public Schools.

Can we justify killing anyone, police or citizen, because the Ferguson police force was charged by Eric Holder with excessive traffic or court fines? What level of hate and where did it come from that motivated the shooter of these two police officers? The Ferguson demonstrators, as with all rioting, are functioning under a continuing mob mentality that can't be reasoned with. All the facts proving otherwise; all reasoning that can be presented will not be accepted. Until these questions can be answered honestly and the knowledge of their foundation recognized, there will be no peace or security for any of our citizens.

Gene N Isom

FROM IKE'S DESK

Free Stuff   **March 30, 2015**

Author unknown:

Emphasis mine. "The folks who are getting *free stuff*, don't like the folks who are paying for the *free stuff*, because the folks who are paying for the *free stuff* can no longer afford to pay for the *free stuff* and their own *stuff*.

"The folks who are paying for the *free stuff* want the *free stuff* to stop. And the folks who are getting the *free stuff* want even more *free stuff* on top of the *free stuff* they are already getting. Now the people who are forcing the people who pay for the *free stuff* have told the people who are receiving the *free stuff* that the people who are paying for the *free stuff* are being mean, prejudiced and racist.

"So, the people who are getting the *free stuff* have been convinced they need to hate the people who are paying for the *free stuff* and giving them the *free stuff* in the first place. We have let the *free stuff* giving go on for so long that there are now more people getting *free stuff* than there are paying for *free stuff*."

He goes on to say that all great democracies have committed financial suicide within 200 and 250 years after being founded. The reason, voters figured out how they could vote themselves *free stuff* from the treasury by electing people who promise to give them *free stuff* in exchange for electing them.

Our Republic started in 1776; that means we have about two decades left before our destruction as a Republic; two decades means twenty years for all of you who are getting all that *free stuff*.

Wake up America!

FROM IKE'S DESK

The fragility of the American voter   April 10, 2015

We have to wonder sometimes if the mental state of the American mind is so fragile that perspiration on the lip, or one bad gotcha, from an adversary reporter will cause the voter to change their vote. What does this say about the knowledge and core values of the American voter?

I'm a firm believer that the importance of political knowledge over the last century has diminished in direct proportion to the increase in welfare assistance. The Progressive movement during the past one-hundred years has done their job well.

As I consider the many similarities between the suppression and control of the lives of our citizen between the governments of our founders and those of today, I have come to believe the citizen of today live under more controls and repression than our founders ever dreamed of. One major difference may be that we don't have government officials billeted in our homes against our will, but government control is alive and well within almost every aspect of our daily routine from the moment we awake until we retire for the day, but of course we have accepted this over time because of its gradualism and of course for our own good.

If every American still had to fend for their lively hood as our founders did, they would be just as concerned with who governs them as they would earning their daily bread. Their attention to the political voting cycle would not start on Election Day, but would probably have been well established months ahead. They would already know who they intended to vote for because of their quest for the *Liberty* they have become accustomed and not be easily suede because of mountains made from ant hills by the opposition party or some reporter looking for fame and fortune.

As our Welfare State grows, our will to govern ourselves diminishes and the control over our lives by government will continue to increase and sink us farther down the Hellhole of Serfdom in which there is only one exit; an educated electorate that realizes that they must replace the current government at the ballot box in November 2016 if they ever hope to recover the *Liberties* guaranteed in our Constitution.

If you agree, pass it on.

FROM IKE'S DESK

Finally, I'm not alone!   **April 20, 2015**

I've been questioning for the past couple of years why someone in Congress has not recognized their constitutional responsibility and brought Impeachment charges against President Obama for his lawlessness and monarchical conduct while in office. It's their sworn Constitutional duty to uphold the Constitution and protect the citizens against tyrannical government actions. Their inaction in this regard proves that they are just as lawless as the President. They should have the courage to fulfill their responsibility to their oath of office and the constituency that elected them. Political Misdemeanors committed by President Obama that could be constitutionally upheld number in the dozens.

The need and want-to has been alive and burning within many congressmen because they have always known it was the right thing to do, but stark fear of the political backlash from the leftwing media has created a paralyses of action on their part and also because he is the first Black President; any white President acting as such, would have long ago been Impeached and probably found guilty and removed from office before their first term had expired. Even the mention of Impeachment has not been heard on the floor of congress to my knowledge, except perhaps late at night during Special Orders for fear of being politically lynched.

Finally, Congressman Ted Yoho of Florida is bringing to the floor of congress a resolution defining the House of Representative's understanding of "High crimes and misdemeanors," the Constitutional standard for bringing impeachment proceedings. I have little hope that it will bring impeachment proceedings against Obama, but it will be interesting to see just which Republican Congressman has the guts to officially sign on and maybe just one or two America loving Democrat Congressmen who remain, will also sign on. This doesn't give me much hope that some action will take place in the near future, because there hasn't been much courage or statesmanship demonstrated by the Republicans in congress for the last couple decades.

The current 114th congress is not a living body, but dies in January 2017. All bills laying before the congress not completed dies with it; which of course means that if any impeachment proceeding should take place, it must start soon and be completed within the next eighteen months, which does not give me much hope of it happening and I'm not sure that this timing is not intentional. It gives Yoho and other congressmen future political cover; they can now say, "At least we tried!" In a real sense all they have accomplished is to let the most corrupt President in the history of our country escape the historical justice that was rightfully and properly due him and his administration.

FROM IKE'S DESK

Pamela Geller's Mohammed Contest　　　　　May 11, 2015

Bill O'Reilly called Pamela Geller's free speech argument about the Mohammed art contest as "bogus." He is wrong; it was "Provocative" as it should have been. To quote Erick Erickson, "History shows us over and over that the moment evil realizes you are scared of provoking it, you have provoke it into action" and that is where we stand today; afraid to confront the evil that the civilized world is facing today because we are afraid personally that we will be attack next.

We must face evil head on and strike back; we cannot sit back and watch it destroy our society because we fear for our own safety. There is a word for such action, or lack of; it's called cowardice.

Rev. Franklin Graham, the president and CEO of the Samaritan's Purse, said "He was discouraged that someone would mock the Muslims, just as he would if someone did so to Jesus Christ." Rev. Franklin Graham is a true Christian that believes in turning the other cheek. Turning the other cheek has not worked in two-thousand years since Jesus Christ walked the earth and it didn't work in thirteen centuries since Mohammed's prophases were accepted by the masses. I will not accept that the more abuse and torture Christians take here on earth will place them closer to the throne of God. Turn the other cheek has never worked and will never deter evil.

Bill O'Reilly is a fence sitter. He is a rude egotistical Pompous Ass, even though I never fail to watch him because of his program content. He looks for every opportunity to throw the left a bone, even when not warranted to help him maintain his number-one status on television. He is highly visible and don't want to provoke the evil idiots in taking his head. So he will say whatever it takes to sooth their evil tempers. However, none of these actions will detour the evil intent of the Islamic jihadist. Nothing will deter the so-called moderate Muslim from their eventual Caliphate. Except for the rare few, the moderate Muslim will never show solidarity with the infidel. They will never be out in mass demonstrating against the evils of the jihadist, but they will be out in mass to witness your beheading.

When I previously pointed out that Obama was a Muslim, I got the response to "Get over it" because there are two billion Muslims in the world and they have done marvelous things for humanity over the centuries. Their contribution to humanity we can accept, it's their cruel and determined dedication to destroying all humanity that does not accept their Religion that we cannot accept.

I'm convinced the reason we find the world in such turmoil today is because too many people have been "Getting over it" for much too long.

If you agree, pass it on, if not tell me why I'm wrong.

FROM IKE'S DESK

Oh what a web they weave!   **July 8, 2015**

Older Americans will remember those days when honesty and the Golden Rule were still taught not only by parents, but also in our schools. We were also taught a little rhyme about deceiving; "Oh what a web we weave when first we practice to deceive."

Most of our current Justices of the Supreme Court are old enough to have remembered being taught that little rhyme. However, somewhere along the way they appear to have forgotten it, or no longer believe and practice it. The rhyme they now go by is; "Oh what a web we weave when first we practice to appease."

Think about it! With each deviation from the basic dictates of the Constitution they create a tighter web into which they cannot get out of without resorting to more appeasement and more gobbledygook opinions to justify their ruling.

This brings me to the point I want to make concerning who will chose the next justice of the Supreme Court. We know it is just a matter of time before one to three justices will be replaced. If that should happen with the next President a Democrat, the future of America as we have known it is over. If it should be by a Republican President, if things do not change within the Republican Party, it will be the same result, because Republican Presidents of the past have more or less played by the rules and approved those that are qualified without regard to ideology. This was a major mistake. The Democrats have never been the least bit bashful about approving the most liberally biased nominee they could find and as long as they passed the bar the Republicans went along. To prove my point all you have to do is remember, and if you don't, do a little research on the crucifixion of Robert Bork.

Even though both parties have nominated and approved Justices that have proven to be more concerned with social justice than the dictates of the Constitution, we have a better chance at a more secure future with a Republican President. That is why the selection of the Republican candidate is so important. They must win the Presidency in 2016 for no other reason than the nominating of the next Justice to the Supreme Court. The future of our America is just that important.

FROM IKE'S DESK

Scales of Justice　　　　　　　　　　　　　　　July 11, 2015

The scales are to symbolize the balance between Truth and Fairness and referred to as the Scales of Justice.

A doctor was recently sentenced to forty-five (45) years in prison for lying to his patients. President Obama has lied to over Three-Hundred-Million American citizen on numerous occasions. I can recognize the truth here, but where in the hell is the balance of Justice?

I think we Americans can no longer rely on Lady Justice to keep her thumb off the scale. What do you think?

FROM IKE'S DESK

The success of the Socialist Democrat Party   August 16, 2015

Why do democrats continue to try to defy the laws of nature? Why do they continue to think that physical certainty does not apply to them or their rules and laws that they pass? They think the law of Supply and Demand serves no purpose and are only words that conservative use to sell the big lie to liberals like them and the uneducated masses. They even would try to outlaw the law of gravity if they thought that a majority would buy it. They know they almost have a plurality that would try. In the face of evidence to the contrary they're determined; no matter how many times their policies have filed, to continuing to take the wrong fork in the road that carries their constituency and the rest of the citizenry along with them to ruin and more dependency.

From the progressive movement of President Wilson of over a hundred years ago to Lynden Baines Johnson's Great Society, their policies have had the opposite effect of that promised. Their failed social engineering policies of the past five decades have cost this nation trillions of dollars in now demolished housing projects alone; other wasted trillions went into teaching generations of citizen how to game the welfare system that has destroyed their will and independence that made them useful idiots of the Democrat Party, especially the black population of our nation who have been effected the worse and don't appear to know it and just keep asking for more abuse from the socialist Democrat Party. Perhaps we can give them credit for successfully wasting more trillions of dollars on dummying down America through their failed education system. Regardless, they must be given credit for their determination and tenacity to change our beautiful America into a socialist state.

The progressives and the Democrat Party leadership have known from the beginning full well the inevitable outcome of their economic and socially destructive policies. They knew they were destroying a healthy and vibrant Republic that provided the most personal Liberty and independence ever experienced by the individual man. They knew this, but their collective thirst for power and control over every aspect of our lives has always been more addictive than concern for any destruction their actions would cause our Republic.

The results of defying the law of Supply and Demand could not be more evident than the results of the disastrously greedy demand for a living wage, i.e., a $15.00 per hour minimum wage in Seattle, Washington. The fact that the price of Burgers has gone up and impacted that element our society that could afford it least concerns them little and the fact that the loss of one-thousand jobs is proof that you cannot defy the law of Supply and Demand. However, the more important statistic is the harm that has been done to those that are no longer employed.

Those hurt the worse are the young people who have lost these entry jobs because they were priced outside the bounds of Supply and Demand. Most of the jobs lost by the increase in the minimum wage were not those jobs that were meant to provide a living wage in the first place; they were not heads of households; they were jobs needed by the youth of our country for the building of self esteem, character and the introduction into the real world of the labor market.

The price of the labor for most of these entry jobs depends upon the availability of labor. The more labor chasing these jobs, the less labor costs. A tight labor market would drive the cost of labor up and the cost of goods and services as well. What's so hard about this that the average Socialist Democrat can't figure out? Ah, but actually they did, but didn't give a rat's hinny about the health of our nation or the individual, only the effects upon their staying in control over the citizenry;

mind and body.

There is little defense against these laws in isolated cases where the socialist Democrat is in full control. A remedy in situations like that being experienced in Seattle is the eventuality of a growing discontent of the citizen directly harmed and those who see the fallacy of such social engineering and make corrections at the ballot box...

The Socialist Democrat Party has just about reached their goal in which no reversal is possible. Our Republic as founded may have one more final chance to correct this downward spiral into total individual servitude; to a point when we are total subjects and the rights of the individual man no longer exists; that choice will come on November 8, 2016.

Wake up America!

If you agree, pass it on, if not tell me why I'm wrong.

FROM IKE'S DESK

Collateral damage be-damned!   November 17, 2015

What a way to fight a war. Would the allies have ever won WWII had they been so concerned about killing one innocent person when their bombers obliterated every major city in Germany? Would Japan have unconditionally surrendered had we not scorched two of their major cities and killed over one-hundred thousand of their citizens with one bomb each? Would Hitler have not sent his V-1 rockets into downtown London and slaughtered thousands of non-combatants if he was not serious about bringing England to a surrender table? Hardly! But yet, Obama and the western world are presently trying to defeat an evil much worse than all enemies of WWII without innocent loss of life.

Folks, it can't be done. If you plan on winning a war innocents will be sacrificed, it can't be helped or expected to deter your efforts to win; your own survival depends upon it.

Just maybe, after this recent attack in France, a few foreign leaders will see the light and through their bold action against a determined enemy will bring our cowardly Commander-in-Chief kicking and screaming into the real world. If Obama's action doesn't appear cowardly, then what would be the one thing to keep him from effectively attacking, or even calling the enemy by their correct name? Does his devotion to the Islamic religion go deeper than we care about the future of our country? Even crazy old Uncle Joe would do a better job at fighting radical Islam than Obama because he was raised and grew up American.

If our country and western civilization survives the next year and with a major change in administrations, we just may be able to fight Radical Islamic Terrorists with a will to win. If you truly love your country and want to see her given a chance to prosper and survive this dark time in history, you better think and work for a major change in administrations in November 2016.

If you agree, pass it on!

FROM IKE'S DESK

Security   December 16, 2015

What is security? My Webster's says: "The state of being or feeling secure; freedom from fear, anxiety, danger, doubt, etc.; state or sense of safety or certainty." We all should know that this definition of safety, security and certainty does not really exist in real life and those that feel they and their property are safe and secure are living in blissful ignorance. We can only try to personally secure ourselves, fortunes and our future as best we can based on our knowledge and the options available to us.

We may try to secure our financial future with Gold, Silver, or other precious metals, but they are all subject to the same pressures of the stock Market or a government controlled by unscrupulous and socialist minded lawmakers. Our gold and silver stashed away in a vault won't earn dividends and is subject to loss or gain by forces beyond our control, or a government that could confiscate our valuables at its pleasure and issue worthless paper in exchange. We can buy a gun for our and our families self protection until the government comes within our homes and confiscates them and only our government is capable of securing us from foreign aggression. We try to secure ourselves in hundreds of ways only to find that the level of security that we seek has never existed and never will. Our security and our Constitutional rights are only as good as the government that rules over us during any given period of time.

Understanding that our Constitutional rights, personal or financial security is always at risk, where can we turn? Unfortunately we must seek our security and safety within the same body that over recent years has been negligent in providing it – Government! Then it becomes obvious that the only source of safety and security that we hope to experience in the future must also come from the government. Realizing our national safety, lives and fortune lies within a whimsical and the unpredictable grip of the government that we elect, you would think Americans would be more judicious with their votes – but not so. They will pinch pennies to choose the best TV their money will buy, but give away one of the most precious and priceless gifts any free people can own without a serious thought - Their Vote!

The American people during the past seven years have just lived through a most perfect civic lesson that could never be provided in any academic setting. By living through the consequences of electing a government that cares little about the Constitution or the will of the people, you have suffered firsthand the fate of carelessly squandered votes.

In one year we will be given another chance to hopefully correct the mistakes of the past two elections. Yes, that's right, we only have one year to reeducate the masses, or at least enough of them to cast a responsible well thought-out vote necessary to turn our nation back toward a sane and constitutionally driven government that will provide as much security and freedom that is humanly possible.

It will not be enough just to write or read about the changes necessary to correct the wrongs of the past, it will take a mental and personal effort by each of us to get off our butts and work toward educating whoever we can that these changes are necessary if we are to once again experience the liberty, safety and security that our brilliant and wise founders envisioned.

Wake Up America!

If you agree, pass it on.

FROM IKE'S DESK

The Complainer! December 23, 2015

I just read an article by whose name shall not be disclosed, of who I know personally absolutely nothing about, complaining about public discourse in general that tells me he is a complainer and not a doer. His gripes are many and thoughtless.

He complains that he does not have input into his party's platform. Ans: Check your mail box.

He complains that his Party does not seek his input. Ans: Open your mail and read it before throwing it into the trash can on the way in.

He complains that he is not consulted when the party elects committee members. Ans: You put your faith in your representative judgment during the voting process.

He complains that his representative is more concerned with top headlines and the latest poll numbers. Ans: Headlines let's your representatives know what's happening and where their concerns should probably be. Poll numbers may very well tell them what their constituencies concerns are.

He complains that everyone is at each other's throat over politics; Ans: He's obviously unaware that's called politics; being civically involved and the process that was necessary to create this great nation!

There is much more, but he ends by asking what responsibility does voters have beyond obeying our laws and Voting. Ans: Are you kidding me?

We all know this individual. He is in every gathering in every location throughout this country. He's sitting across from you at the head table every morning at your favorite coffee nook. He's at every council meeting and is always complaining but never volunteers or becomes personally involved. He and millions more with the same mental deficiency is exactly why our country has an anti-American President sitting in the Oval Office and a traitorous and cowardly Republican Party that more or less agrees with him…

The Best of 2016
(From Ike's Desk)

With the following posts I've tried to lay out an almost day to day coverage of the Republican campaign for President of the United States of America during the year of 2016 with only an occasional mentioning of the Democrats because there nomination process was virtually over before it began; only one real choice and that is Hillary.

While reading the various Posts you should find two definite themes during the entire year of 2016. First: My belief that Donald Trump as a candidate for President of the United States as the Republican Nominee was the wrong chose; that has not changed with his victory as President Elect, but could very well turn out to be exactly what our country is needed at this time in history. The second is that I proudly and unabashedly lay bear my personal political philosophy that I have lived by for my entire adult life for all to read.

You will read time and again my reasoning throughout these posts why I disagree with the election of Donald Trump as President of the United States and why I think by all standards of previous Presidents, Senator Ted Cruz would be the best choice for our head of State.

The very first Post from Ike's desk was on January 7, 2016, titled "The Awakening!" Just maybe Trump's election will become that spark that I was looking for that will ignite the flames of patriotism once again within the bosom of every American loving citizen. Just maybe his style of governing, although crude and corrosive in many ways, will still result in turning our economic and social decay back toward a government "Of the People, for the People and by the People," and away from our currently corrupt run government. Let's hope!

FROM IKE'S DESK

The Awakening! January 7, 2016

Admiral Isoroku Yamamoto supposedly said after his attack upon Pearl Harbor seventy-four years and one month ago today "I fear all we have done is to awaken a sleeping giant and filled him with a terrible resolve." There isn't any existing record that he ever made that famous quote, but there is a record that he was certain that the resolve would produce a terrible counter attack by the sleeping giant.

Although war was raging all over the world, we were still setting on the sidelines and involved only through our Lend Lease Programs, but that sneak attack by the Japanese on Pearl Harbor that sleepy Sunday morning was indeed an awakening. I was at a Boy Scout Jamboree at Pere Marquette State Park in Illinois that Sunday Morning and remember it well.

The American people immediately came together with a Great Resolve as Yamamoto had feared and assassinated him on April 18, 1943 by a flight of P-38 fighter aircraft that shot down his bomber just off Bougainville Island in the South Pacific while he was on a morale building tour. We know whose moral was boosted by his death on that date. This also happened on the one year anniversary of Col. Doolittle's raid on Tokyo. Yamamoto's fears and prediction had truly come to pass.

If there was another awakening or moral building event in America's future it has not been evident for the past seven years with the exception of the assassination of Osama Bin Laden and if the truth was known, Obama was pulled into that decision kicking and screaming and would never have allowed the Navy Seals to kill him if he could have prevented it politically. It may very well end up being the only claim he can make for his legacy. His Obamacare is about to be destroyed; what's left?

If there is another awakening within our future it will have to come from a gigantic wave of a rebirth of patriotism. The same patriotism that created this great nation over two-hundred years ago; a great hunger for personal liberty without hindrances from thousands of bureaucratic and government laws and programs that are stifling the productivity of a free people; an awakening of a realization that our government and many elected officials have become the enemy of the people and have lost sight of their sworn responsibilities; a knowledge that we the people are responsible for what we have created and we the people will have to correct it. As the corruption of our government continues, the rebellion by the citizens will grow until civil unrest will create unhealthy confrontations between the people and our government. This must end with the election of November 2016.

During the next twelve months we have a chance to once again show our resolve to reverse the weak and productive robbing capability that our government has become and especially the Obama administration and produce the kind of government that once again recognizes the job creating potential of the individual entrepreneur; allows the free market place to dictate policy and remove the socialistic tendencies heaped upon the citizenry by a government that deceptively creates programs the people do not want or have input. This can only happen with an awakening within each liberty loving American citizen determined to do everything they can as individuals and to prove that the American people are still capable of demonstrating once again another Great Resolve.

If you agree, pass it on.

FROM IKE'S DESK

Cruz – His Team?   **January 16, 2016**

Cruz has been accused of not being a Team Player – Their Team, meaning the GOP. Cruz's team is not the GOP, it's the constituency that elected him; the conservative movement that is rising up in the country with a vengeance for change; a change back to the basic roots that molded and form the greatest country the world had ever known. That's the team that Cruz represents, and for most of us conservatives, to hell with the GOP Team that is joined at the hip with the Democrat Party. Many of those now supporting Donald Trump would have nowhere to go but to Cruz' team if Trump should stumble, and I'm still hoping that will happen soon. The following is from the Streiff (Diary) dated Jan 12, 2016:

"Cruz wants to recover that mood and maybe also those particular Reaganite ideas. So his appeal is exceptionally nostalgic. The future figures in it only as the scene of a recovery of a lost time, a time that worked. And the Obama years (and here and there also the Bush and Clinton years) figure as a disastrous detour. This nostalgia strikes me as the core of Cruz's message, essential to his appeal. Many conservative voters, especially older ones (who are predominant) surely find it easy to love.

A nostalgic case against a corrupt establishment is an argument for a better establishment. But Cruz's case is nonetheless also genuinely populist, and in an interesting way. His vision of political change is rooted in an enormous faith in the power of public outrage. Cruz implies that by getting people angry about where the country is headed, he can channel great democratic energies toward changing direction. What we are missing, he suggests, is a leader who can get us angry about the right things. Cruz believes he is that leader and that his time in the Senate has proven it."

I agree, although Streiff uses the word nostalgic frequently that may give readers the assumption that Ted Cruz and his followers are just dreamers; wishing for a past that cannot be recaptured. Not so! The nostalgia is for a time when the country functioned as a Republic and not as a social experiment by a leadership with monarchial powers; a time when the three branches of government each protected their constitutional authority jealously; a time when the Supreme Court ruled on the legality of law instead of changing the law and becoming the instrument of social change; a time when financial security and thrift were important to our lawmakers. Those are just a few of the nostalgia that Cruz's team long for. They are not just dreams, but with hard work by team members they can and will become reality.

Wake Up America!

FROM IKE'S DESK

The Same God   January 19, 2016

Do Muslims and Christians pray to the same God? Well, not in the mind of this lowly one who professes to be a Christian, although lacking the devotional fervor that all devout Christians should display. However, in my opinion the answer to the above question is a resounding No! Muslims and Christians do not serve and pray to the same

God. Christians worship the God Jehovah, Muslims the god Allah.

Not being a scholar of religion or a serious student of Christianity as I should considering the many hours of being forced to endure a sore butt from sitting upon un-cushioned hard wooden pews during my youth by my Christian mother, I can say little, but do believe that the Christian God is a triune God, made of the Father, the Son, and the Holy Spirit. The Islamic God Allah is an absolute single God and anyone who claims he is anything but a single entity is guilty of blasphemy and therefore must be punished.

When we pray to the Christian God we do so in Jesus' name. Muslims do not believe in that God. So how are Muslims and Christians praying to the same God? The next time I hear a supposedly intelligent (go along to get along) politician tells me that Muslims and Christians pray to the same God, I'll scream Hell No! Christians pray to a heavenly God and Muslims pray to – well, I just don't know what God they pray too? I know they scream "Allah Akbar!" "God is great!" while their sharp knives slice through the throats of Christians while cutting their heads off. If that's their God they are praising for allowing them to commit such a ghastly crime, what God are the Christians praying to as their throats are being cut at that moment? It can't possibly be the same God that required the Muslim to slaughter the Christian in such a heinous way.

Do Muslims and Christians pray to the same God? I don't think so? What do you think?

If you agree, pass it on.

FROM IKE'S DESK

Sarah, you have broken my heart!   January 20, 2016

Sarah, I've watched and studied your political life from the moment you became the Governor of Alaska. I read your book and of course voted for you and – that other guy - during the 2008 Presidential election. During the eight following years I watched you push many conservatives to victory with your Pizzazz, vigor and energy; your honest fervor for the conservative movement. However, with your endorsement of Donald trump yesterday I was shocked by your switch from a Principled Conservative to a Reactionary Conservative; at least I've always considered you principled and dedicated to the honest conservative movement; the movement to reverse our countries downward spiral into socialism...

I would have bet money a week ago that you would have endorsed Ted Cruz because of his proven record of being a Principled Conservative as I thought you were. It is so easy to abandon a ship you may think is sinking because of the massive political waves that are washing over it. The total forces of the left as well as the Republican establishment handicaps the principled conservative candidate considerably and will cause their support to search for calmer waters. But that has not caused you to slink away from your support of the right causes in the past. Sarah, you were the bedrock of support that could very well have guaranteed a victory in Iowa for Ted Cruz. The support you may have now generated for Donald Trump could very well have gone to Ted Cruz.

Ted Cruz and his supporters will now have to work double-time in Iowa if they are to become the victors. A victory for Ted Cruz in Iowa will change the direction the Republican search for the White House will take; a defeat for Cruz could mean that Donald Trump could very well be the Republican Candidate.

Sarah, you may have started believing that the predictions and forces of the left combined with the republican establishment that Cruz cannot beat Hillary is right and that you are willing to switch and support a Pig in the Poke, if it could possible win the White House and that's possibly what our country will get with Donald Trump. I could be wrong Sarah and you right, but my feeling is that you like Mike Huckabee, has sold out your conservative values for personal political gain.

Regardless of who becomes the Republican candidate, every living breathing human being with a brain the size of at least a Bee-Bee had better get behind that Republican Candidate if they ever hope to reclaim our country from the clutches of the Liberal/Socialist movement that has literally torn it apart and now with your shocking support of Donald Trump Sarah, you have broken my heart.

FROM IKE'S DESK

Three white shirts   **January 25, 2016**

Note: This was scheduled to be sent the morning after the State of the Union Message, but another more important subject took precedent and this was never published.

As we sit and observe what is revealed before our eyes and listen to words that are being spoken each of us have thoughts that vary in countless ways, although they may be similar in many. I was looking at the three faces before me during the State of The Union Message and couldn't help but wonder what was going on at that moment in the minds behind the three faces. We have known these three faces for many years and their particular politics and therefore we can only assume we can tell what their thinking at any given moment of the address.

As I watched the television I saw three white shirts, three ties of different color and three dark suits behind which lies three hearts beating at various rates that nourishes three brains functioning in three different political directions.

The brain in front is struggling hard to concentrate at the moment on the delivery of words being read from a teleprompter with as much oratory skill as possible with little thought at the moment; only the importance to his ego that the delivery be perfect enough to conceal their meaninglessness.

The brain to the rear right is struggling to maintain its composure and not reveal through a facial expression the contempt for the brain standing before it, or the Monkey Grinders Brain sitting to its right.

The brain to the rear left is trying desperately to control its emotion and working extremely hard in hopes of not revealing itself as the Organ Grinder's Monkey and wondering when the brain to its left will force a change of expression upon the face of its owner.

And, what of my brain you ask? Well, as you can see it works in mysterious ways as well.

FROM IKE'S DESK

Do we need more debates? January 30, 2016

Debates have become promotional campaigns by the networks for the purpose of generating millions of dollars from their advertizing. One or two major debates may serve a good purpose, but after that they are for the general welfare of the networks alone.

I've sat through all the Republican debates to date except for one, but after the last one, I've come to the conclusion that there is no need for more; they have said it all. With a few exceptions of the sickum questions; those designed especially to pick a fight between candidates, there were few that were new and most fell within the same subject area. The answers we heard have been repeated so many times by the candidates that a serious voter and viewer should now know not only the words coming, but the cadence and intensity with which it well be delivered.

I personally do not expect the moderators to try to make the debate more exciting for me, or for ratings, by picking fights between individual candidates on the stage. For me, the moderator's objective to create a p---ing match between candidates is for promotional purposes of the moderator alone. This has been proven by the coverage they receive during the news cast the next day and we hear as much, or more about the moderator than we do the candidates – maybe a slight exaggeration here.

Election after election we always hear of the huge numbers of supposedly voters who have not made up their minds before they are to vote. It has been said that there are up to thirty percent in Iowa that have not made up their minds who they will vote for. I don't buy this at all and most know well in advance who they intend to vote for and in all probability will not change their vote. Those that claim this are either newcomers to our political process, stupid, or an ego searching for publicity.

It has been said that if Trump does not lose the Iowa caucuses, he will not be stopped and will probably be the Republican nominee. I believe that may very well be true and if so, this is one more item added to my "Why we're losing our country list."

FROM IKE'S DESK

Conservatism!   **February 5, 2016**

During the political fight going on between the Republicans and Democrats for the presidency, the word conservatism slips from the lips of Republican leadership as easily as if they truly believed in conservative principals as understood in today's political concept. They speak the language because they know that the American citizens are hungry for conservative principals to once again govern our nation, otherwise there would not be a Donald Trump.

Republican leader's voice conservative principals with ever breath, but their actions are totally contrary to everything conservatism stands for. They sell the virtues of conservatism to buy your vote, but really have no intention of governing as such. The Republican Leadership has proven this in the past by giving Obama everything he wanted and will continue to govern to the left in the future.

Conservative leaders in this country are so hungry for the Presidency that they will sell their souls for it and are now working feverishly for a less conservative candidate because they have lost faith in the cause of conservatism and are now convinced that only a moderate can win this November. This belief has now permeated throughout the hard core conservatives within this country as well and they too have now abandoned their principals by the dozens and are willing to settle for a less conservative candidate because they have bought into the big lie that a true conservative candidate cannot win, but how would they now, it hasn't been tried lately. The electorate is ready and asking for a conservative leader and would have one if the true conservative leaders of the past (you know who they are) remained true to their principal. Hopefully, the will of the people will overcome their cowardliness and betrayal and persevere.

Every time you hear Republican leaders mention conservatism, ask yourself why they are not practicing what they preach. If they were true conservatives, Ted Cruz would be receiving their support. He is the only solid conservative candidate in the race for the presidency and that is why the leadership is doing everything they can to destroy his candidacy. They know with Ted Cruz in the White House, much of their control and power will be diminished, but they believe they can control the moderate established candidates running with the exception of Trump, who would be a disaster not only for the conservative movement, but our nation as a whole.

There is no doubt that a Rubio, Kasich, or a Bush President will be a great improvement over what we have had the previous eight years. They are moderate conservatives and will give away almost as much as they get when dealing with the democrats. The decline of the Christian faith will continue at a rapid pace and the reversal of the socialist movement will be unnoticeable or much slower with these moderates than it will be if Ted Cruz becomes president. However, there has not been one republican candidate running that would not have made a great improvement over the Obama disaster of the last eight years, or the Democrat we may get for the next four. The damage created by twelve years of Obama will never be reversed until our government runs out of other people's money and there are no more free stuff to give away. When that happens…?

Wake up America!

If you agree pass it on!

FROM IKE'S DESK

The RNC??? February 7, 2016

Does the RNC have so little brains that they think the Liberal networks will in any way enhance the standing of the Republican Party or the Presidential candidates by allowing these networks and so-called moderators to conduct these debates? By now they have to know that these moderators are intent on creating as much mischief and mayhem with their questioning as possible for Republican politics in general and the candidates specifically.

Reince, are you really this stupid? If you really had the best interest of the Republican Party and the candidates, you would insist that an equal number of Democrat debates must be conducted by Fox news and the moderators must be staunch conservatives, i.e., Shaun Hannity, Glenn Beck, Mark Levin and maybe Bill O'Rielly, except he is too much the fence rider and wouldn't want to rile his standing with the left. The debates and candidates of the Democrat Party must be equally challenged, otherwise no more Republican debate on ABC, CBS, NBC, and CNBC. CNN, or any other liberal network. Period.

I watched the debate from beginning to end and made notes immediately at its close:

Christy - overall had the best night. If there was a winner, he was it.

Trump - Never hurt or helped him. Partially wrong on Emanate Domain.

Bush – Had a better night than the last debate, but no movement.

Cruz – Had a good night, but nothing outstanding except he and Carson acted as the only grownups in the room.

Carson – Was Carson.

Kasich – May have helped himself.

Rubio – Was definitely the loser if there was one.

I'll have to wait and see how far off I am from what all the pundits will be saying for the next day or two.

FROM IKE'S DESK

Trump Won, but did he? February 10, 2016

Trump was the big winner last night in New Hampshire with a 35 percent of the Republican votes; at least that is the headlines this morning on all the T.V. networks. But did he really win? If Trump only received 35 percent of the republican votes cast, that should immediately tell all the networks that 65 percent of the republican voters did not want him as their candidate. That tells me he may not have been the real winner after all; 65 percent sounds like a winning number to me.

What if Trump had been up against a single candidate such as Hillary Clinton? Would 16 percent of those that voted against him last night have changed and still made him the winner? I don't think so! As long as the number of Republican candidates remains high, it will be difficult to determine just how popular Trump really is. As the number of Republican candidates narrows through attrition, we will get a better idea of just how popular Trump's wild-assed promises really resonates with the Republican, Independent and Democrat voters, who will not be voting Democrat this November.

As we approach the South Carolina primary we see that Trump still holds the lead over other Republican candidates by a large percent. However, we can see that the one biggest surprise to the pundits was how well Cruz did in New Hampshire. They were not expecting him to do that well without the evangelical numbers that do not exist in that state. This will be an entirely different story as we go into the southern Primaries. As Kasich said last night; "Tighten your seatbelt because things are going to change," and my hope is that Trumps numbers will start dropping relative to the number of Republican candidates dropping from the race.

FROM IKE'S DESK

Justice Scalia has died! February 13, 2016

I just heard on the tube the death of Justice Scalia. The world does not yet know what a disaster has just befallen upon our way of life with the notification of the death of our most conservative Supreme Court Justice. The death of this great jurist is a tragedy in itself, but his absence from the bench at this moment in time is a great blow to the loss of freedoms the American citizen may very well feel for several generations to come.

With the Democrats and Obama still in power the timing of his death could not have happened at a worse time. The Oval Office is dancing with glee at this moment over the possibility of appointing his successor that will cause shock waves throughout our society and over shadow all election and campaigning activity within the government for the foreseeable future.

If there was a time that our government needed a strong Republican leadership; one that hasn't been evident for the past ten years, it is now. If the leadership in the senate does not step up and counter the left wing radical nominee by President Obama now, then there will be no hope for our Democratic republic.

God help us all.

FROM IKE'S DESK

What were you watching?   February 14, 2016

If you were watching the Republican debate last night and enjoyed it for the entertainment, you got a freebee. The clown was at his best and once again proved that he is not ready for prime time.

Donald trump's conduct on stage last night was that of an overbearing bully and egotistical interrupter and name caller. He called both Cruz and Bush liars on several occasions when they pointed out his record of supporting liberals and the democrat Party. His inflated ego could not control his mouth when any other candidate had an opportunity to speak. His disgusting facial expression every time the camera was on him had to be a real turnoff by many viewers. In other words, he acted the real buffoon last night, but not the least bit funny, and definitely proved not to possess the demeanor of what we expect of our President.

I believe the other candidates conduct themselves in a respectful manner even when they were defending themselves against a tyrant. Kasich was one adult in the room along with Dr. Carson although I don't see either improving their position much. Rubio was his normal verbally fluent self as words rapidly flowed from his lips as if they were coming from a machine; however there was another real gentleman in the room that conducted him with a proper decorum that demonstrated he was ready to conduct the affairs of state and that was Ted Cruz.

FROM IKE'S DESK

**If he'd only had a road to
Damascus moment**   February 20, 2016

There is not a day that this President doesn't continue to prove he is not a true American. He continues to insult our traditions and the

American way of life. If I could meet him face to face I would have to ask him why he chose to be not only the enemy of the Black citizens, but the American people as a whole during his time in office. I would have to ask him if he was so filled with hate for the American way of life when he became President that he couldn't see what greatness he was capable of as our first Black President? Of course I'll never get that chance, nor would I accept the offer to meet face to face with Barrack Obama if the chance was offered. I believe it's proper to show open disrespect to the office of President if the holder of that office cannot show equal respect for the American people.

What would our nation and the world be like today if Barrack Hussein Obama would have had a Road to Damascus moment the minute his hand was laid upon the same bible that Abraham Lincoln used to take the oath of office.

FROM IKE'S DESK

What does Hillary Know? February 23, 2016

Why does Hillary continue along as if she will never be indicted? She's either delusional or has an inside track as to exactly what the future outcome of her lawlessness will be. A normal mentally balanced thinking individual that has committed crimes against the State hanging over their heads, as Hillary has, would act very different defensively. Is this an act, or is she really so mentally unbalanced that she really believes she has done nothing wrong. Now that says a lot about the mental state of someone who would make such a claim. However, she is not alone. Trump claims he has never had to ask forgiveness of anyone, not even God, and both are trying to become President of the United States. We should all be asking for God's help right now considering these two choices.

As we all continue to speculate on when and if the FBI will recommend an indictment against her crimes, she acts as if she already knows exactly what the outcome will be. Could it be that she has been told of the charges and the conclusion? Has Obama assured her of an immediate pardon the moment the indictment has been handed down, or before he leaves office? If so, is she really delusional enough to continue to campaign and believe that the citizens are stupid enough to elect her President? Ah, forget that, we know the answer.

The power to pardon is one of the least limited powers granted the President of the United States. He has the authority to pardon anyone that has been charged with a crime against the United States of America, but not states or local crimes. Of course this is all speculation and knowing there isn't any love lost between these characters, Obama just may want to see her in broad pinstripes.

The excuses we keep hearing from the media is that new charges are coming so fast that the FBI doesn't have a chance to charge her because of new investigations. That's nonsense and the FBI has known for some time that she has broken the law and is holding off a recommendation of indictment for political reasons only. The FBI is no more than a puppet on a string and the stings are being pulled from the Oval Office regardless of what the excuses given by Director James Comey. The failure of the FBI in this case to act timely is another reason for the anger building within our citizenry; they are convinced that the people can no longer trust our departments of government to fulfill their sworn responsibility nonpolitically and fairly.

FROM IKE'S DESK

we finally had a debate   February 26, 2016

I hope you all watched the Republican debate last night, because if you didn't, you missed great entertainment. It was really the first time that

Donald Trump was not allowed to be the big overbearing Gorilla in the room. Last night he was left with nothing but funning faces and index fingers pointing in the air and trying to push his antagonists away on both sides. His face and hands were more entertaining than anything he may have said. In spite of Blitzer's attempt to control the debate, the candidates decide they would determine who and when to speak.

Rubio and Cruz both went into that debate determined to expose Trump for the charlatan that he is and I believe they were very successful for the first time. It's unfortunate that they didn't gang up on Trump in earlier debates; the poles of today may be reflecting a different standing. There were two more candidates there that served themselves well, but did little to improve their standing in the polls.

Rubio's attacks were mostly for purposes of ridiculing Trump and Cruz on substance. Cruz' attacks were on Trump's inability to prove where he has ever demonstrated an ability to govern and preserve our Republic and the Constitution; this is what all elections should have been about.

Trump's claim that not one Senator has endorsed Cruz has had me puzzling over the very same question? Is there really not one seated Senator that does not believe as Cruz, or have the courage to publicly say it and endorse him; if this is true, then there is very little hope for Cruz' presidential bid or the future of our Republic?

In four days there will be the big test for all those remaining in the race for the Republican Party candidate. On Wednesday not much will have changed and I think the top three will still be standing until the middle of the month. After winner-take all primaries there should be little doubt as to who the Republican Candidate will be. If there remains doubt after March, then the talk of a brokered convention may have merit, but this is highly doubtful.

Cruz still remains the best hope for the future of our Republic!

FROM IKE'S DESK

A New Party　　　　　　　　　　　　**March 7, 2016**

The Founder's Party

I am proposing that a new political Party be formed in the United States and the name should be the Founder's Party; a party that takes us back to the basics of all that was right with America at its founding. I don't believe the new name should be the conservative Party, although very appropriate, but already has negative tags attached. The American Party would be good, but American encompasses the entire American continent and not just the United States to which the party would relate.

The symbol of the new party will not be that of a stupid stubborn jackass, or a large lumbering prehistoric animal that can be easily ridiculed by all opposition, but one that is a head shot, or cameo of an American 1776 Patriot; one that all Americans can find a common thread or relationship with; not a symbol that can be easily ridiculed by opposing points of view.

The motto must also be neutral and constitutionally orientated that pledges faith and allegiance to its application; an inherently expressed covenant between the people and the party.

The Democrat Party turned left and deserted their constituency many years ago, but was open and above board about it. The Republican Party was more dishonest and sneaky in their attempts to deceive the people into voting for them. Now after years of broken promises by the Republican Leadership, the people are tired of it and now desperately grasping at the Pied Piper, but hoping for a different outcome. It ain't gonna happen!

It is obvious that the time is right for a third party to come along that the citizens can once again have faith in that will provide the leadership that they are so desperately in search of; to provide a leadership that is determined to preface all government action and laws on their constitutionality and not social engineering; a leadership that understands that our Constitution has to provide equal opportunity for all citizens without prejudice or favoritism; a leadership willing to fight for and appoint judges at all levels of the judiciary that believes in the intent as debated, and not of a particular ideology.

If such a party is founded and the citizen convinced of its conservative orientation, meaning the purpose for which our country was founded, I believe they will swarm to its causes and could very well fill the rolls and the party could become a major player in a very short period of time, because we are now going through a tumultuous political period ripe for change.

Think of the disillusioned Democrats that feel their party has deserted them; the Republicans that feel their party has betrayed them; those that felt they had to switch to independent because they could no longer associate themselves with the two major parties; they should welcome a chance to join a new political party if it's based on the concept of a word rarely heard or used in recent years – the Constitution!

We know that change is hard and always resisted. We become comfortable in doing it the way it has always been done even when we inherently know it's probably wrong. It's human nature to at first look negatively upon anything that upsets our routine and forces us to rethink that which has become accepted, right or wrong.

I'm suggesting that all disillusioned citizens let both parties know that there is a rebirth of patriotism within the citizens of this country and they're not going to take the social decay and mismanagement of our

Constitution and country any longer.

Wake up America!

If you agree, please pass it on to your friends as well as your senator and congressman. There has to be a Party for the true conservative American patriot that believes our country as founded is worth saving.

FROM IKE'S DESK

Does early voting serve us well?   **March 9, 2016**

We now know that Louisiana early voters went overwhelmingly for Trump, but votes cast on Election Day were evenly split between Trump and the other candidates. So what does that tell us?

It so happens that during the time I was standing in line for early voting in the State of Tennessee, I was wondering about that very thing; if those in line were as positive as I that they are voting for the right person or would some have changed their minds by Election Day and of course then it would be too late. I'm now convinced that question needs to be explored further.

How often have we heard since voting has begun that thirty to thirty-five percent have not made up their minds twenty-four hours before casting their vote. If this is so, that means those late deciders are casting their vote with information about the candidates that early voters were not privy to. The voting patter between the early and late vote proves this, as in the case of the voting in Louisiana and I think future voting patterns by state will prove the same.

So the question should be asked is the convenience and simplification of the early voting process unfair to both, the voter and the candidates as well as a detriment to the country overall? And the only answer I can come up with is, absolutely!

It is becoming apparent that Trumps popularity may be diminishing slightly for several reason and one of them has to be the revelations of his political history and shenanigans that are becoming more public everyday and available to those voting on Election Day and not to early voters.

Political sage Newt Gingrich, who I believe is the most astute within the Washington political establishment today, claims Donald Trump's followers will not be deterred at this stage of the political process and if that is so, and Trumps victory margins are diminishing, it has to be due in a large part to later information that was available only to those undecided twenty-four hours before Election Day.

Regardless, the convenience of not standing in long lines on Election Day will not be changed because we know that convenience with today's citizen is more important than knowledge and the country will continue to suffer the consequences of a uniformed electorate.

Wake up America!

FROM IKE'S DESK

Briefly! March 10, 2016

I'm making this statement immediately after the debate before any of the normal political pundits have a chance at tell it all wrong; "The Republican debate last night was the most civilized and informative debate so far during this election cycle." The Moderators ask question that were perfectly designed for information without promoting themselves, or purposely designed for picking fights between the candidates. Each candidate was given time to answer the questions and for the first time, Trump's interruptions and gesturing was held to a minimum. All previous debates should have been conducted in this manner. CNN did a great job.

Who won? Whoever on the stage you were planning on voting for! By my objective analysis it was no doubt, Ted Cruz!

FROM IKE'S DESK

Early voting, bad idea! **March 28, 2016**

Where have you read this before? This was published on March 25, 2016 On Headlines News. A blog that publishes headlines news from around the country. I do believe From Ike's Desk is getting around; well, probably not! Murdock did however add more information why early voting is a very bad idea that is worth reading. Ike

By DEROY MURDOCK March 23, 2016 1:56 PM

GOP primary voters in Arizona did the Republic a great service last night: They demonstrated the idiocy of early voting and confirmed why it cannot be scrapped soon enough. Real-estate tycoon Donald J. Trump won the Republican contest with 47.1 percent, as of this writing, with 96 percent of precincts reporting. Senator Ted Cruz of Texas followed with 24.8 percent of the vote. In fourth place, Governor John Kasich of Ohio took 10 percent of the ballots. And, in third place . . . Senator Marco Rubio of Florida with 13.4 percent. Dr. Ben Carson took fifth with 2.7 percent. These 16.1 percent of voters may have included die-hard Marcoites and Carsonians who loyally stuck with their men after their candidates departed the race. However, the vast majority of these were probably early voters whose ballots had been dropped into precinct boxes as far back as Wednesday, February 24 — one month ago. Most of those voters probably feel like fools today, having squandered as much as four weeks ago the opportunity to affect the three-way race among Cruz, Kasich, and Trump. Rather than allow citizens thus to make fools of themselves, America simply should catapult early voting atop the ash heap of history. Instead — what a concept! — voters should vote on Election Day. On that occasion, they should choose from among the candidates who actually still are running for office. Protest votes should be counted, of course, if drop-outs still appear on ballots. However, such votes should represent conscientious objections, not the pathetic echoes of choices rendered meaningless by subsequent events. Voters who cast their ballots on February 24 knew nothing about the GOP debates on February 25, March 3, and March 10. They voted four days before Trump stumbled into hot water by very, very slowly distancing himself from the admiration of former KKK Grand Wizard David Duke. And, for whatever impact it might have had on their decisions, these voters were unburdened by knowledge of ISIS's deadly attack on Brussels the morning of yesterday's canvass and Tuesday afternoon's stomach-churning disgrace: President Obama doing the wave with Cuban dictator Raúl Castro at a Havana baseball game, even as innocent Belgians bled and expired on gurneys after being attacked by Islamo-fascist scum. Early voting also means that ballots sit around, night after night, in storage while awaiting tabulation. The reality of, or potential for, vote fraud is obvious and chilling. Over several weeks or even a month, ballots can get up and walk away, never to be counted. Conversely, corrupt ballots can be stuffed into unguarded ballot boxes in the middle of the night. Even if nothing fishy happens, the mere suspicion of fraud can taint genuinely elected winners as the stale fruit of a shady system "manipulated by the 1 percent" or "manhandled by union bosses" — take your pick. Such doubts about the legitimacy of voting results can cast destructive shadows on America's elected leaders and erode democracy, more swiftly than the Colorado River carved the Grand Canyon. — Deroy Murdock is a Manhattan-based Fox News contributor and a media fellow with the Hoover Institution on War, Revolution, and Peace at Stanford University.

FROM IKE'S DESK

Corruption Corrupts April 4, 2016

Sarah, you have broken my heart!

I have never known someone that I've always considered a staunch conservative and have defended in the past, fall from grace as fast as Sarah Palin. From the moment Sarah Palin endorsed Donald Trump for President her station as a past conservative leader plummeted to near irrelevance. She hitched her wagon to the tongue of an egotistical pompous mouth that thinks he is qualified to be President. She threw away her hard earned conservative standing among true Conservatives for future fleeting fame and fortune. Her core values and principals were sacrificed in an instant of very bad judgment, probably never to be regained. I can't help but think of how great she would have appeared today with her conservative standings intact had she accepted her past role as a conservative and supporter of Ted Cruz.

This morning I watch a video of Sarah's nineteen minute speech in Wisconsin and I was shocked not only at the reception she received, but also her attempt at desperately trying to sell Trump's worthless ass to those attending. As pointed out, also by others, she received only three applauses during her entire speech. The first was when she was introduced; the second was when she praised the Green Bay Packers football team; not once for anything she said about Trump. The biggest applause received was when she ended her speech and walked off the stage. Sarah, there is no doubt you have lost your Mojo. Hopefully you can reclaim your conservative image, but it will be sometime in the distant future.

Lately I've been reading much about the destructive power of Donald Trump and his ability to bring out the worst in those who associate with him. The self-esteem and image of those who hitch their future to

Trump's wagon fall precipitately. The images of Palin, Carson, Christy, Huckabee and other prominent persons are very good examples of damages to images that will never be viewed as they were before Trump. I can't help but believe that many of them will start realizing in the very near future, especially if Trump loses the nomination, that they have made a very serious mistake. It's sad but very true that association with corruption corrupts.

FROM IKE'S DESK

The Republican Nominee! April 5, 2016

Last night I witnessed an articulate, honest, and informative Republican candidate fluently answering every question ask of him with an unapologetic candor. It was heartwarming and reassuring to know that we still have at least one that will not sell out his principals to buy the allegiance of those who may disagree.

Ted Cruz spent the entire hour last night answering the questions put to him by Megan Kelly and members of the audience. Not once did he use the normal time fillers used by the other leading candidate while helplessly searching for the answer that will sell, or that the audience may want to hear; he expressed his true beliefs without glorified adjectives and never once repeated himself.

Ted Cruz unabashedly defended his Christian faith and the principals upon which his life is based. He easily answered this question and set those minds to ease that may have been erroneously led to believe of his intent to establish a theocracy if he should become President. Christian Presidents abide by the Constitution, secular Presidents, as has been proven, do not!

I defy anyone to name one of the seventeen original Republican candidates and those of the Democrat Party that could possibly be as open and honest and solidly firm in their beliefs and in defense of the Constitution than those of Ted Cruz; there were several that came very close.

Today there will be three candidates fighting it out in the State of Wisconsin; one is irrelevant but which of the other two that may win can very well be the turning point of this election concerning the Republican nominee. Who wins Wisconsin today could very well tell us if the Republican Party is headed toward a contested convention or if Donald trump could win the necessary number of delegates to settle the question.

It is my hope that Ted Cruz wins the Wisconsin Primary today which will indicate that we will probably end up contesting who will be the nominee on the convention floor and Ted will eventually end up winning the nomination, because Donald Trump and his lack of temperament and qualification to be President will become too well known by then.

God Bless America!

FROM IKE'S DESK

The selling of ignorance! April 13, 2016

The selling of ignorance in this country is running rapid from those that have been proven to be behind the curve in politicking. Trump and his supporters believe it is unfair that the candidate that received the most votes during the primaries may not win. They do not take into account that the votes for several candidates make up 100% of the total vote. In Trumps case, he may have received more votes than the other candidates did individually, but at the same time more votes were cast against him than for him; so at that point he loses. So who is it that is being treated unfairly; Trump if he is not given the nomination even if hasn't earned it, or the majority of voters that voted overwhelming against him?

Trump and his supporters appear totally ignorant of the fact that no candidate, no matter how many votes they may have accumulated up to the convention if they hadn't reached the majority of 1237, has no bearing on winning until the majority of delegate votes has been cast on behalf of the candidate on the convention floor. It only means at that point that you are still competing.

Maybe to clarify: Too many people, and I think Trump is really not that dumb, confuses the number of votes accumulated during the various state Primary Elections and the number of delegate votes needed to win the party nomination to run for President. The only relationship between the two is the number of votes won at the various state primaries can lead to the number of Delegates earned going into the convention.

Trump, his followers and many supposedly bright people on television appear to consider a system that has been in place for over 150 years, with little tweaks here and there, unfair to all those presidents that accepted and were elected under this system in the past. If it were truly that unfair, it would have been changed years ago. All those candidates that have lost over the years were not as stupid or as demagogic as Trump and many of his national known supporters and would have changed the system long ago.

Trump was totally unprepared to place his name in contention for President. He didn't have an organization in place to know how to use the system to win delegates. He thought his overwhelming egotistical personality was all that was needed to become President. His son's didn't know either. They were too dumb to know they had to change their registration from Democrat to Republican in time to vote for their father – which they can't. There is no telling how many more of the Trump clan that cannot vote in the New York Primary for The Donald. But I'm sure that system is considered unfair to The Donald also. It's obvious that anything that works against The Donald just has to be unfair because he is entitled and has won more votes in the Primaries. Fortunately for the majority, it doesn't work that way!

A Thought? Could it be possible for Trump to have a minimum plus a couple extra delegates (1240) going into the convention and still not win enough to be the nominee on the first ballot on the convention floor? YES! And if so should his supporters riot, NO! It's only the Democratic processes at work. They just can't understand the democratic processes that have been in place for many years. What it means is that the majority doesn't want him and for very good reasons; they finally got to know him.

Wake Up America!

FROM IKE'S DESK

Ignorance ContinuesApril 14, 2016

My post dated April 13 appears to have pointed out just a *smidgen* of the ignorance that continually comes from the mainstream media on a daily basis. It is this ignorance and compliances with it that is continuing to fuel the flames of dissention within our society today.

If you happened to be watching the O'Rielly Factor last night, I hope you were one that was alert enough to catch another reason why our country no longer believes in the concept that the knowledge of rules and order really matter to a civilized society. O'Rielly and his two guests appeared to agree with Trump and many other uniformed so-called intelligent people that the candidate with the most votes should win. O'Rielly suddenly questioned where they came up with the 1237 delegate count in order to win? His two guests, Kyle Kondik and John Yob looked blank and neither took the opportunity to straighten him out, because it was obvious that they didn't know either. It happens to be exactly one-half plus one of the total delegates (2472) that will be voting at the convention; it's called a simple majority. I'm sure O'Rielly had a sheepish look on his face later when someone pointed this out to him.

To accept anything less than a simple majority of the total delegates voting to win the nomination for the Republican Party is totally out of sync with everything that has been right about our country from the very beginning. For a majority of our citizens to accept anything less than a simple majority, as many polls are showing, proves the social decay that is slowly eating away at the foundation that our country was built on. For the RNC to now accept Trump as the winner if he gets at least 1100 delegates instead of the simple majority of 1237, as many prominent politicians are accepting, turns our Democratic Republic and principles we have been governed by upside down. They have now disenfranchised the votes of the majority of delegates that worked hard and at great personal expense to represent their voters at the state level. If what some are proposing happens, a minority of stupidity has now won!

On another note I must mention the great coverage given to Ted Cruz and his family last night on CNN. I'm truly sorry if you missed it because you would have witnessed a great First Family in action that would make America proud again if Ted Cruz should win the Presidency. The difference between the characters of the top two candidates is striking.

Wake up America!

FROM IKE'S DESK

Fair Rules for delegates April 17, 2016

Megyn Kelley presented another ridicules question that creates more wonderment about the smarts of some of these FOX News Hosts. She asks a delegate from Michigan that was bound to Trump if delegates should be bound to their candidate after the first ballot if their candidate does not win? Do you understand the results of this question if the rules were set in the affirmative and did Megyn really realize the result of her question? The delegate only answered that she was sticking with her candidate, but ninety percent of you reading this have already realized exactly what the results would be – the delegates could never produce a winner no matter how many times they voted if they were not freed after the first vote.

The purpose of the political party convention is to select a nominee to run for the President of our country; the rules that are in place are there to facilitate that purpose. The only way a nominee can be chosen is by unbinding the delegates after the first failed ballot to produce a clear winner by a majority. Otherwise there would be no need for a convention in the first place just give the nomination to whoever has a plurality of delegates. If there were only two candidates from the beginning, that would work and which candidate had a plurality would be the presumptive nominee by state Primaries, but still would not be the nominee until a majority had been voted by the delegates on the floor of the convention. Of course with up to seventeen candidates receiving votes over the Primary voting period a candidate that holds a plurality does not necessarily have a majority and to award that candidate the nomination disenfranchises a majority of the primary voters. The purpose of the convention is to elect a nominee by majority of delegates voting on the floor at the convention. That's the way of a Democratic Republic.

The citizens of this civically deficient country are starting to get the civic lesson they have forgotten, or never received in the first place whether they like it or not. The contentious nature of a spoiled brat that goes by the name of The Donald; a product of the Republican establishment, just may have created a positive effect after all, but at a very high price.

I believe that one of the best lessons that could be taught to the citizens of our nation at the moment would be for a national coverage of interviews with delegates of various states to tell how they were chosen and the ordeal they endured to become delegates. Do you hear me O'Rielly, Susteren, Kelly and Hannity; you four that have been promoting the dissention so heavily, whether intentionally or not. Let each delegate explain their personal election process concerning the hard work and personal expense to be elected as a delegate to the convention to represent their state. After hearing what each has to say, I believe most citizens will agree they were not bought and sold by party leaders and there isn't Hanky-Panky being played to deny any candidate a fair chance at becoming the nominee of their party. However, Trumps ago will never accept anything that tells the world that he is a loser and in his mind it just has to be unfair.

Here is the short version of the rules to become a delegate to the national Republican Convention for the state of Tennessee: Any person that wants to become a delegate to the convention must submit their name to the Secretary of the State no later than December 17 of the previous year. Along with the affidavit must be twenty-five names of registered voters along with several documents for each name. If everything is in order your name may be placed on the ballot within your district. On March 1, the citizens of Tennessee voted for those they want as delegates. It's a simple Democratic Process. No Hanky-Panky! The delegates will exercise this patriotic endeavor at their own personal expense.

My opinion, as with many, is that Trump was never serious of becoming President in the first place and has often used the out "As long as I am treated Fairly" and has used every lame duck excuse since as to why he doesn't win everything –FAIRLY, because he really doesn't want it and will continue to use every destructive tactic available to make sure he cannot win the nomination at the convention. He knew of the method to elect delegates at the state level but purposely refused to fight for them so he could claim the system rigged against him. His oversized ego is trapped and surprised by the arduous furor he has created in his followers and now doesn't know how to stop the chaos he has created. The only salvation (out) available to him is to lose at the convention. Trump is a phony! He really isn't suited for, nor is it desirable, for Trump to be living in Public Housing.

FROM IKE'S DESK

Where is Jethro Bodine?   April 26, 2016

I have a very real concern that our citizens and especially the media no longer have the ability to add numbers together and come up with the right answer, or know the difference between MAJORITY and MINORITY. We all know that even Jethro Bodine of the Beverly Hillbillies knew how to cipher, but it appears to be too complicated for our politicians and political pundits concerning delegates.

Let's start from the beginning and see if we can't explain the difference. It will be difficult to get through their thick sculls, but I'm going to give it a try by starting from the beginning of the delegate selection during the primary process and work through it:

1) Every delegate was elected or chosen by the MAJORITY during their state primary election; a very democratic process.

2) Accumulative when all the primaries have finished voting there will be 2,474 delegates at the convention to vote for the candidate to be the nominee of the Republican Party That have been selected by a MAJORITY of Republican voters; a very democratic process.

3) Along the primary voting process the several candidates have all received a number of votes. The winner of each primary rarely wins the MAJORITY of votes cast by the voters of that Primary; which means the winner actually won by a minority of votes. That means that a Majority of voters did not want the winner – Got It? But it's a very democratic process.

4) After all states have finished their Primaries hopefully one candidate ends up with a MAJORITY of delegates, a simple MAJORITY of 1237 to become the nominee going into the convention. If there is no candidate with a delegate count of 1237, things get a little more complicated – we now have a contested Convention; rules for this too is a very democratic process.

5) At the convention there will be a first floor voting by the 2,474 delegates to see which candidate can come up with 1237 votes (a simple majority) and become the nominee. You must remember at this time that the candidate with the most delegates coming into the convention was still in the minority. More voters to this point voted against the leading candidate than voted for him; in this case Trump. He has yet no claim on the nomination simply by have more delegates or a bigger voter count than other candidates coming into the convention. The MAJORITY still has not decided who will be the nominee. That will be decided by a very democratic voting process.

6) The rules for voting on the floor of the convention have been in place for many years and accepted by many candidates. The rule is that most delegates are free to vote for whomever they choose on subsequent

votes if no one gets the 1237 on the first vote. This is a very necessary rule otherwise a winner would never be chosen. The MAJORITY that has been voting against Trump over the period of Primaries now have a second chance for someone else. They must continue to vote until one candidate receives the magic number of 1237, and that very well may not be Trump. If so, he was not chosen as the nominee by a very democratic process and has absolutely no right to throw a tantrum and sic his goons into rioting.

7) We know at this point that about sixty-five percent of the Republican voters do not want Trump and have voted against him. Considering a large number do not want Donald Trump as their President, why would O'Reilly and so many other prominent pundits think he should be awarded the nomination simple on the count of delegates above another candidate when it takes 1237 to win and most voters don't want him? They apparently don't understand the difference between minority and majority and feel their Donald should win regardless of what the MAJORITY have voted for. Oh where is Jethro Bodine when we need him.

FROM IKE'S DESK

Bring it on! Let's get it over with! April 28, 2016

I am fed up with these threats of chaos and riots if Donald trump, his cult and the mainstream media don't get their way and give this spoiled brat the nomination even if he hasn't earned it. These comments by Rush Limbaugh, O'Reilly and others are tantamount to instigating the riots they suggest may happen if Trump does not get his way. What happened to responsible speech and expression by supposedly intelligent individuals? Do they not know their speech is directly contributing to the chaos they appear to be concerned about, or do they really want for the sensationalism that they claim not to want; that is the question that has been on my mind for some time now and I have to question their motives? We know the media thrives on chaos and if they can't find it they are evidently determined to create it.

I've been told to watch out for what I wish for! Well I'm still looking and wishing. I didn't get my wish when McCain became the nominee in 2008 because he wasn't a conservative. I didn't get it with Romney in 2012 because he too was not a conservative. Now it looks like I'll not get it again with another disaster by the name of Donald Trump as the possible nominee of the Republican Party and he is Democrat with a capital "L" for liberal. There is however still a slight glimmer of hope in the possibility that I will get that wish with a true conservative by the name of Ted Cruz.

The last hope may start or end on next Tuesday, May 3rd. If trump wins it may be over. However, if Cruz wins there will be new life breathed back into his campaign and the agony continues a little longer.

Hopefully, Trump will not have acquired the 1237 delegates to close the deal before the election. Trump and others apparently do not understand that he doesn't own the nomination until he earns it on the floor at the convention. No one can take from Trump what is not his in the first place.

Our country has been exceptional because of our peaceful transition from government to government until now. Trump and his cult are determined to turn us into something no better than another illiterate Banana Republic if they don't get their way. Let the demagogue and his cult bring it on and get it over with so we can start over from the ashes of what was once a great nation. Maybe this time we can keep our citizens civically educated.

FROM IKE'S DESK

Our founders and the Constitution   April 29, 2016

I always marvel at the wisdom and knowledge our founders possessed as they debated the creation of our constitution. If you really want to know who and what they said during the debates, you need to read "The Constitutional Convention;" a narrative history from the notes of James Madison. While reading, you will become involved and no longer be living in the abstract, but will become a part of the convention.

When completed, they knew it was not perfect and changes would need to be made from time to time and built in a perfect amendment system that required slow and deliberate thought. For the last half century at least, our elected representatives have slowly unraveled and discarded this most perfect document for free men to live by. With the continued selection of Supreme Court justices with about as much care and attention as selecting a television at Wal-Mart, our liberty they fought so hard for has been eroded to a point that they wouldn't recognize and the future looks very bleak. The election coming this November may very well be the last chance we have to stop our downward spiral into social decay and a dark and dismal future.

It really troubles me that so many of our citizen do not recognize the deterioration that has occurred by liberalism and their political agenda that has slowly destroyed our federalist system that allowed the greatest chance for all our citizens to live free and prosperous as our founders intended. They cannot recognize the dangers lying within our leading candidate. They are so p----t off at the way our representatives have screwed up our country that they'll now settle for the devil as long as any change can be made.

There is only one candidate that has consistently advocated for what the founders intended when they debated the Constitution. There is only one candidate that is knowledgeable enough of the Constitution to adhere to it as the guiding principal for the governing of our country. There is only one candidate that has never wavered in his dedication to uphold those principals upon which the Constitution was founded that has made our country great in the first place. That candidate is Ted Cruz!

Wake up America!

FROM IKE'S DESK

Slouching Toward Gomorrah   May 3, 2016

A few months back Trump started out on a small ego cruise around the pond in row boat and now finds himself trapped at the helm of a cruise ship headed toward a reef and don't know how to stop it or turn it around. What started out as an ego trip he has unintentionally, or not, turned it into an unrepairable disaster for the Republican Party and the destruction of the greatest nation the world had ever known.

What I'm saying here is not hyperbole, but the facts as they are developing right before our eyes. The poles as we read then tell us that Trump most likely will be the Republican nominee. Should that happen they also tell us he most likely will not beat Hillary or the Democrat nominee in the general election and continued control of the house and senate may also be in doubt.

The results those two events will undoubtedly result in actions by the extreme left progressive movement, after one-hundred years of trying to finish the job of destroying our country as we have known it by continuing the Slouching Toward Gomorrah. For those of you unfamiliar with that term should read the book by that title written by Judge Robert Bork in 1996; revealing the results of Liberalism and its destructive nature and was he ever right! His nomination to the Supreme Court was rejected because he was a Constitutionalist on the scale of Justice Scalia.

The only hope for the continuing of our nation as a free Democratic Republic is to stop Trump at all cost, even if he gets to the 1237 before the convention. That number only makes him the presumptive nominee before the convention. The sixty percent of Republicans that do not want Trump as their nominee have every right to try to convince the delegates on the floor not to vote for him. The majority still has rights also!

FROM IKE'S DESK

Do Principles Conflict? May 4, 2016

This was written in early April but held off until we knew who our nominee would be in the general election and now we probably know it will be Trump. There's still a chance, but...

We hear much about Principles lately, but what are Principles? Principles, knowingly or not, govern our course of action concerning how we react to certain condition that we are confronted with in our daily lives. The most current conflict may be one of voting for someone whose political philosophy we may not agree with or believe may be the lesser of two choices. Again, it may be that we must choose between two conflicting principles which can be troubling if we feel very strongly about both. One may be not voting for a nominee that we feel unworthy of our vote and if we uphold that principle and not vote, we may be violating a principle much more important to the future of our country.

The dilemma for many may come from a promise of never voting for Trump under any condition should he become the Republican Nominee and allow Hillary to become President, or, vote for Trump to help insure our country is spared the horror of four more years of Obama; either way one Principle must be violated.

No rational thinking Republican voter should lose any sleep over which of these two principles to violate. It is no doubt harder to vote against the principle in front of you at the moment because of the visibility and timeliness of the person or event. However, being concerned with the future required more brain power and as individuals we have to actually think it through – heaven forbid! The future of our country is only speculation at this point and the destruction created by a wrong decision cannot easily be felt or visualized and may use up more brain power than some of us are willing to dispense with. Therefore I fear too many Republicans will stay home in November to uphold their thoughtless principle of not voting for Trump and may very well end up losing the election and their country by violating a larger and more important principle for failing to vote to save our country from the clutches of an administration run by a known Socialist/Democrat Party.

The easy out for all republicans and the future welfare of our nation would have been the nomination of Ted Cruz on the floor on the convention and make our job so much easier to defeat the evil forces of the left to win the Presidency. However, the people, right or wrong, have made their choice and now we must work hard to convince every responsible thinking citizen to get behind Trump and make sure he has the votes necessary to defeat the Democrat nominee this November.

It is better to take a chance on a Pig in the Poke than a known disaster as the Liberal/Socialist Party regardless of who may be their nominee. Either way I'll now have the working title for my next book. "I told you so! Damn It!"

I don't have to wait for Trump to serve a year or two as President before predicting the outcome of his administration no more than I did before Obama was elected in 2008 and 2012. I predicted with disastrous accuracy his administration before taking office on both occasions as well as I know Trumps. Either way, if the good Lord's willing and I'm around in January 2018 I hope and pray the title of my book turns out wrong and I won't have a reason to tell you – I told you so! Damn it!

FROM IKE'S DESK

A Disastrous Tsunami   May 7, 2016

A deadly tsunami has swept across our nation and washed out all vestiges of sanity and common sense. Americans that claim to be republicans have voted to award a Liberal Democrat Demagogue that was never a republican and has never had to ask for forgiveness or say he was sorry, the nomination of their party. Much of this movement was led by prominent individuals that were once staunch conservative leaders that always fought back vigorously against the socialist progressive movement. They were Governors, Senators, Representatives and leaders within the entertainment and news media that just a few years ago would have fought with all the energy they possessed, to prevent this egotistical demagogue with his destructive power from ever gaining the most powerful position in the world.

We now know what a disastrous consequence has befallen the Republican Party and our nation by the Republican Leadership for not standing up and protecting the people from the evil Obama and Democrat Party. We also now see how easy it was for Jim Jones of the Peoples Temple to convince over 900 people to drink the poison Cool-Aid, or, David Koresh of the Branch Davidians to convince his followers to parish in a fiery death. All Trump had to say was I'm going to build a great wall and Mexico will pay for it, and with that he suckered millions into his cult and had the nomination cinched. Trump apparently possesses that same cult magnetism to persuade enough to make him their new Messiah and to a fate not only to be experienced by his followers, but by also the sixty percent of responsible republicans that voted against him and the rest of the nation. Now the majority of voters must join ranks with the cult or suffer four, maybe eight more years under a socialist government; which may in the end be better than what were fighting for.

What is 'is' and we're all in it together whatever that may be. Now we must work hard for this Pig in the poke to bring about the best possible consequences of this mess created by the corruptive actions of Government leadership of both parties; one by intent and the other by cowardliness and inaction; and possibly intent.

God help us all!

FROM IKE'S DESK

Justice May 9, 2016

What does the word Justice mean to you? Does it mean fair play and honest treatment; does it mean authority and power? It may mean a lot of things too many people, but hopefully it brings to mind our court system as administered within the confines of our constitution and when we think of the court system, our first thoughts should be centered on the Supreme Court system and the reasons for this should be obvious.

There are few activities that we become involved in during our day to day activity that has not been influenced in some way by court action. In some cases our normal accepted way of life has been turned upside down, whether in the area of religion or social activity and most of it has happened within the past four decades. The degradation of Christianity started in 1963 by basically outlawing all Christianity in our public schools and has expanded to just about every government entity since. The Supreme Court has not served the Christian or our moral society well and has contributed to the continued degradation of our social standards. This of course is working well for our secular society but overall the social and religious health of our nation is suffering tremendously.

If we look back and take a close examination we see that most of this was for the benefit of ten percent or less of our society; the concerns of the majority of ninety percent didn't matter. The Supreme Court has unnecessarily turned thousands of years of accepted social standards upside down for the benefit of misguided equality and political correctness for the few. They have forced the majority to capitulate normality to an elevated abnormal minority. This goes far beyond normal equality of treatment.

We are now in the process of electing our next President, Considering that one Supreme Court chair is open presently and there's a possibility, considering the ages of the justices, two or three more positions may open within the next four years. Keep in mind that justices of late are no longer nominated on the basis of their adherence to, or, the textual understanding of the Constitution makes our consideration of who to elect, considering the choices, a loose proposition, but never the less an extremely important one.

It is almost a certainty that if another Justice with a total disregard for the Constitution when ruling upon issues before the court as Justices Roberts and Sotomayor has done, then you can kiss the first few amendments of our Constitution goodbye. Christianity in a short time will only exit between the walls of your house or your church building. The mire mentioning the name Jesus Christ in public could eventually get you thrown in jail. Don't ever doubt that this will not, or cannot happen, when we already know there are powerful forces at work already trying to make it illegal to deny Global Warming. It only takes a *very few* wrong people in power in the Supreme Court and our government to make it happen. Verse yourself on what's going on presently in North Carolina and you can see the power the President and government has over every aspects of our lives. There is no doubt it could likely happen during Hillary's term in office if she should win the Presidency this November. It may also happen if Trump becomes President, but there remains that slight outside chance of a miracle if those of greater wisdom around Trump can persuade him to nominate a true Constitutionalist. Well? It could happen! But if those two become the nominees of their party, what other choice do you have? Think about it even if it boggles your mind. The future of our country is too important for you to ignore these issues.

Wake up America!

FROM IKE'S DESK

Who's in Charge?   May 11, 2016

There are so many supposedly ex-conservatives that wouldn't give Donald trump the vote for dog catcher a few years ago are now falling all over each other to get the best cabinet position in his administration should he become President. In the Army we used to call these individuals – Brown Noser's. They're constantly trying to outdo each other to see if they can't do the best job of defending this sorry ass we've allowed to become the presumptive nominee of the Republican Party. The argument they all use, and the only one they apparently feel they can legitimately use in the face of all the negatives, is that he has won by more votes than any past candidate in recent memory; and that is true, but not because of Trump and his proven ability to govern a nation, but because of the miserable performance of our government during the past eight years.

Last night on the Megyn Kelly Show, I watched one that I've always held in high esteem, smirkingly try his best to buy his way into the Trump cabinet by once again using this vote count argument to convince the audience that Trump is a legitimate candidate that can win the Presidency this November. Huckabee has used this same argument but the other half of the story is always left out by Huchabee or any other sell-outs to the conservative movement when trying to sell Trump. They don't add that he also received the most votes against any candidate in recent history. All his high numbers prove is that more people voted in recent history, not that Trump was so much better than other candidates of the past.

Trump has legitimately won his position as presumptive nominee at this point in time and that fact can't be denied, but the process of establishing a nominee by the Republican Party is not over. With so much dissension between Trump and the Republican Party I suppose it is proper to ask, who is in charge, Trump or the Republican Party? At this point if you are able to open your mind to clear thinking for a few seconds you would understand it is the Republican Party that is responsible for choosing the nominee they believe has the best chance at winning through the process they have established for that purpose – Delegates at the convention will choose the nominee. A presumptive nominee is guaranteed nothing, although they usually turn out acceptable to the delegates, but not always as we know and this may be another one of those exceptions.

Now let's get real. Trump won a little over eight million votes and over one million more than his closest rival. However, there were over fourteen million that voted against him out of a total votes cast of twenty-two million. That heavy percentage against the Presumptive nominee has never happened before. Now we're talking about Republican Party votes here and it's the Republican Party that is supposed to accept their nominee at the convention that they think will win the Presidency in November. When the delegates at the convention have to weigh all the factors of the high negatives of Trump, plus the odds of him beating the Democrat nominee; coupled with a huge majority of republican voters not wanting Trump as their nominee, why would they vote for him on the floor of the convention? Must the Republican Party accept the defeat that is presently before them simply because a minority voted for Trump, or do they encourage the delegates to choose a better nominee? That is really the responsible thing to do if indeed things continue to worsen between now and the convention.

Now who's in charge, Trump or the voters of the Republican Party? After all, we are supposed to try to win nationally, not just the primary process!

Wake up Republicans!

FROM IKE'S DESK

Who's got our Back? May 13, 2016

When you stop to consider that for the past eight years we have been governed buy the most corrupt and incompetent administration and a worthless Commander in Chief of our armed forces, along with the weakest congresses in the history of our country, why haven't our enemies been more aggressive in taking advantage of our incompetence? As Admiral Nimitz said after the battle of Midway during WWII, are we that good, are just lucky, or something to that effect. At that time there was no doubt in the minds of the American people that yes, we were that good; but today?

Today with our entire nation involved in the most disruptive and chaotic political process in recent history, coupled with the incompetence of this administration, we better hope that there are still those of our military and Defense systems that are staying on top of their jobs and not being distracted by this turmoil. Our security and the future of our country depend upon it and I hope it's not that we are just being Lucky.

Yes, our military still has our back, God Bless them! At least that part of the military in which Obama has allowed us to keep. Wasn't it reported that we ran out of bombs as one reason we couldn't make as many air strikes against ISIS that we wanted? That knowledge alone should be enough to scare the hell out of every American citizen. Do we still make bullets in America? Just think, it was reported that Cleveland is not ready for the Republican Convention because China has not shipped them their riot gear! Is the equipment so much cheaper from China that we could no longer find a U.S. company to make our own riot gear? Have we really become this weak?

Wake up America!

FROM IKE'S DESK

Free the Delegates! May 16, 2016

We must encourage the Rules Committee of the Republican Convention to allow the delegates to vote on their wish, or their right, to be unbound on the first ballot and it should be done as soon as possible. This would give all delegates time to converse and allow their voters of the various states to give the feedback necessary for the delegates to make a responsible decision.

With a large number of prominent republicans unwilling to vote for

Trump, a situation that could very well destroy the Republican Party for years to come, or forever, a recourse should be available to the Party as a whole. Also with Trump winning by a minority and such a large number of republicans dissatisfied with Trump as their nominee; it's only right that the majority has some means to at least see that justice is done. Of course if you're a Trump supporter, your definition of justice will be different than that of Webster, or of mine and the majority that voted against Trump.

This situation has come about because of the very large number of republican candidates that were originally running for the republican nomination. Under passed primaries there were only a very few candidates and the presumptive candidate had won by a majority of votes cast and therefore precluded the situation in which we now find ourselves. Trump has become the presumptive nominee with a minority of votes, creating the split and dissatisfaction within the Republican Party, which leaves us with several unsavory choices.

One choice would do absolutely nothing and let the chips fall where they may. If that is the choice we make, we may be condemning the Republican Party and the Citizens to the ash heap of history. On the other hand we could at least let the delegates find the nominee they think could best represent and save their party and the country.

I am firmly of the opinion that the second choice would be the most beneficial to the party and the country overall. Yes, there is that threat that Trump will sic his rioters on us and create havoc for a period of time if he were not chosen, but this nation has come through riots before and we will survive them in the future. The delegates may very well if freed end up selecting Trump as there nominee and if that happens, so be it; he was elected fairly by a majority and the majority has spoken and those that don't want Trump probably would not create a riot as Trumps voters appear prepared to do, but still may not vote for him and overall that would be unfortunate for the Republican party and the nation as a whole.

What do you think?

FROM IKE'S DESK

The Trump News Channel   **May 23, 2016**

The Fox News Channel has become a very big disappointment to me and for many of their viewers. When it first came on line people hungry for truth and honesty were drawn to it like a magnet and it soon became the biggest network in the country; why, because people instinctively knew they had been fed a liberal doze of crap by NBC, CBS, ABC and CNN networks for years and the biggest crap spreader was none other than our national Granddaddy, Walter Cronkite, who was a phony; he was the biggest liberal of all. From that point on I rarely if ever watched complete news casts on any of the other four liberal TV channels that had been poisoning the spongy minds of our nation for the previous forty years.

Many of us knew we were being had by the liberal networks, but had no other choice but sit and scream back at the tube, until the available of FOX NEWS. I remained a faithful FOX viewer until a few months ago when it became obvious that FOX was in the tank for Trump; they had succumbed to the persuasive powers of a true Demagogue, Donald Trump; it had now become the Trump News Channel and finally others are beginning to see it also and are starting to write about it more often.

The first of the FOX NEWS headliners to succumb to Trump Mania and join the cult, and I might add the last that I thought would, was Sean Hannity, then Greta followed by O'Rielly. Kelly held out the longest, but even after Trump had trashed her, she is now starting to fold.

To watch these stars of the FOX NEWS topple like a row of dominos is sickening to their once conservative followers. Now with FOX NEWS all stars also among the fallen media greats, there is nowhere to go but to the web. The Web and Talk Radio are now the last line of defense against the radical left and the Trump cult, although different political parties and theoretically opposed, they are none the less, equally disastrous to the social well being and longevity of our Republic.

When Ted Cruz folded so suddenly, which is still puzzling, it appeared that all hope was gone. As long as Cruz hung in there, the chance that Trump would not get to the magic number before the convention was still a possibility. If that had happened, I am convinced Trump would not win the nomination, but now with each passing event, the likely hood of stopping Trump from becoming the nominee appears less likely. The hope for a historical and patriotic awakening by responsible delegates at the convention is unlikely, but still remains the last sliver of hope for the true conservative and the future well being of our nation. The pressure on the individual delegates must continue.

I doubt that a survey will ever be conducted of the individual Trump delegates to see if they still would vote for Trump as their nominee. Since the Republican Primaries started three months ago, many of those early chosen delegates now have gotten to know Trump and can see that he is not a man of his word. Everything that was once promised and accepted as fact, has now become a suggestion or negotiable. Many can now see he is not to be trusted. It would be revealing to see what percent would no longer vote for Trump were they not bound? I'm convinced the percent would be high enough to prevent him from becoming the nominee.

As the old English proverb goes, "If wishes were horses, beggars would ride." But I don't think it has ever stopped us from wishing or praying for that miracle.

FROM IKE'S DESK

Trump's Vice-President? June 2, 2016

There has been much speculation about Trump's pick for Vice-President as there has for his Supreme Court nominee and both choices will tell us about everything we need to know about Donald Trump after the selections have been made; how conservative Trump may be as well as how he will govern if indeed he wins the Presidency. These two choices alone will go a long way toward the persuasion of many who are now dead set against voting for Trump. I for one may look upon Trump for the first time as having some hope for the future, with both of these choices; not just one.

Those whose names that have been released as a possible Supreme Court pick has so far received high makes from just about every conservative leader. There isn't much a conservative could complain about if any one of those named would actually become Trump's nominee. Of the top three named today as his top picks for Vice-President doesn't cause chills to run up and down the legs of most conservatives, with the exception of possible General Flynn. Senators Croker and Sessions will cause nothing but yawns from just about all voters and are as about as exciting as watching grass grow. Now on the other hand, the name Newt Gingrich that is being tossed around for the number two slot in my opinion, which isn't worth much in some corners, would be a great choice and accepted readily by almost all republican voters that have any knowledge whatsoever of Newt.

In the past I have spoke of Newt Gingrich in glowing terms as possibly the most articulate and knowledgeable politician in Washington during the past thirty years. Any conservative dealing in facts and not personal animosity will agree that Newt would be a perfect pick for Trump as his Vice-President. I really believe Newt Gingrich as Trump's pick for Vice-President, along with the right choice for the Supreme

Court would convert many Never Trump voters to change their minds. If trump wants to be President he better wise up quickly and start acting Presidential, which may not be possible, but making the right picks for the Supreme Court and Vice-President may ensure his Presidency.

Just a note: I have asked who is Trump's hand motion choreographer? Is it being taught or natural? If it's being taught, it's distracting. If it's natural, then it appears to be expressing the great egomania within the man. Just a thought!

FROM IKE'S DESK

Who is out of step   June 2, 2016

When you watch Soldiers marching down the street during a parade and there is one soldier out of step, he will stand out instantly no matter his position within the troop. As the troop leaders calls out the cadence and his left foot comes down when the leader calls left, is he the one out of step, or is it the rest of the troop out of step? In this situation it would be hard to convince most observers that the lone soldier is the only one in step and everyone else out of step, because no one listens anymore and most often judge a situation with little thought, or by eyesight only. That is how Trump became our nominee; without rational thought.

I believe that many of us that are unwilling to skip to get out of step with the Trump cult and join their mania feel we are in the same situation as that lone soldier marching to the correct cadence within the troop. Although we are among the sixty percent republican majority that don't want trump as our nominee, we are treated like we are the ones out of step with those caught up in Trumpmania. Those of us that are instep are marching to a cadence called out many years ago by our founders and the concept of the Constitution they created which of course is contrary to a concept in which Donald Trump has demonstrated time and again, he doesn't understands, nor will abide by.

As we continue to see the chaos created by the Donald Trump's candidacy and presumptive nomination, I believe we are just beginning to see a long hot political summer before us filled with riots and more riots, right on up to the Republican Convention in hot July if changes are not made.

In this country we all have a right to demonstrate in a peaceful manner. We do not have the right to destroy property or disrupt other's rights to also demonstrate their right to hear what others have to say. Free speech has always been one of the major hallmarks of our society and must be maintained even if authority must bust some sculls to do it. We have been living in a very unhealthy political correct mindset for the last few of decades and it is now time for it to stop and to restore law and order.

Have you ever wondered why it's only the left that demonstrates unlawfully, and we know who the left are? Going back as far as the Vietnam era we see that those on the left, and not necessarily the extreme left, have been the ones demonstrating unlawfully to quell free speech; and whose speech is it that is always being silenced? Yes, it's always the right, the conservative speech, that must not be allowed to be heard and particularly in our colleges and universities. Can you think of or name a time that the right has ever demonstrated unlawfully to prevent others from hearing free speech? Probably not, and if it has happened, it would have been very rare by misfits the left enjoys classifying as extreme right-wing.

The sixty percent of republicans against trump have never demonstrated unlawfully against Trump although Trump has played every dirty trick he knows to silence any and all opposition. These are the same tactics Obama used to gain political advantage while climbing to the

White House. It will be unfortunate and the future of our country will suffer greatly for it if we end up with another Obama or Democrat for President. There has to be a better choice, and that better choice must occur legally at the convention, and must not be attempted by a third party run that will work only to the advantage of the Democrats.

Wake up America!

FROM IKE'S DESK

Early voting and cultism June 8, 2016

It is starting to become clearer each day as this campaigning season continues as to why States should never allow early voting. We know it saves time and money for the state, but is overall detrimental to both the voters and welfare of the country as a whole. We now know that the pattern of voting changed considerable from the start of early voting in many states and the date of their primary and that change can only be attributed to knowledge gained during the interim. This alone may or may not have changed the outcome of who wins the nomination of either party, but does prove that early voting has been extremely unfair not only to the many early voters, but the Party as a whole.

The effects of cultism throughout the primary voting period can be devastating. The early driving force of the demagogue can overpower all rational thinking during the primary voting period that results in a nominee that is totally unfit to be the President of the United States, as we are now witnessing. Because of the cowardly behavior of the GOP Leadership to not fight for the people against Obama's social and economic destroying policies and impeach this incompetent when they had a chance, they created a situation where the people would grasp at anything that appeared to fight for those ideals they believed in and were ready for a cult leader like Donald Trump. But now, they are beginning to see that Donald Trump is not the messiah they thought they were getting, but it's too late, he has won the required 1238 delegates necessary for a majority which now makes a correction extremely difficult and fractural.

This period of time between the last primary and the convention is becoming a period of remorse by many Trump supporters. Human nature being what it is, most that are now seeing their serious mistake will hunker down and look for every weak and inexcusable reason to continue to defend a nominee they know is wrong for the Republican Party and the country. A perfect example was the debate last night on Fox News Network between Bill O'Reilly and Charles Krauthammer concerning Trump's racist remark about judge Curiel and the need for the judge to recues himself from Trump University lawsuit. Krauthammer refused to let O'Reilly resort to his habit of talking over the top of anyone that may be making points. This is the first time I've seen that sheepish, I've been exposed and whipped look, on O'Reilly's face when the exchange was over. It is impossible to defend the indefensible even for O'Reilly who has been a supporter of Donald trump from the very beginning, but pretends he's being neutral and continues to try to convince us that he is also fair and balanced. It was easy for Krauthammer, because he was dealing in facts and that's something that is in short supply by Trump defenders, even O'Reilly.

Trump's slogan, "Make America Great Again" is as about as phony and on par with a Socialist's slogan, "Change You Can Believe in." Phony slogans are for lazy thinkers and that's about as kind as I can make it.

Wake up America

FROM IKE'S DESK

"There you go again!"   **June 14, 2016**

"There you go again," Mr. Make Believe President, turning a national disaster into an opportunity for total gun control. Instead of responding like a real President by assuring the people that your administration is going to do everything within your power of assuring the people you will provide the leadership they desire, you used the slaughter of those massacred to resort to the familiar and radically worn out childish cliché of Gun Control.

President Obama, Hillary and every other radical left wing politician are not stupid. They know that the Gun Control they preach is only incremental steps for eventual total elimination of private ownership of firearms of any kind. They are intelligent enough to know that the taking of firearms from the citizen will not stop what happened in Orlando. What they really know is that an armed citizenry is a threat to their overall agenda of full control over the citizens.

The Second Amendment is not for the sole purpose of personal self defense as O'Rielly and others have said. The founders made that a part of the Constitution for defense against an over reaching and tyrannical government. That's right, they knew the Constitution they had created could only last under virtuous leadership and was suited for no other kind. When the Bill of Rights were added, the first ten Amendments, a few years after the Constitution was written, they specifically wrote the Second Amendment for defense against a despotic leadership.

Armed citizens will never completely stop what happened in Orlando, but being conscious of the fact that it can happen should make for responsible decisions to insure the citizens are as safe as possible with armed security. More responsible citizens armed is the only thing that can effect this type of horror if only slightly, but, how much is even one or two lives worth? We can only speculate as to what the final count would have been had the business hired one or two trained and concealed armed guards to be among the attendees. Maybe eventually owners of business of this type will have to provide that security by law.

Wake up America!

FROM IKE'S DESK

Tomorrow is the 4th of July   July 3, 2016

Tomorrow is the 4th of July, a date we have been celebrating now for 240 years. Perhaps we should pause for a moment during this holiday weekend during our hot-dog chomping and beer drinking long enough to give thanks for the many sacrifices that have been made during that period for the right to celebrate as we chose. There will be parades and celebration to provide the entertainment of many with little thought at all as to why their being entertained. Older citizen and veterans will stand in reverence as the flag passes by, but most will sit not caring or no longer knowing what they're supposed to do.

It makes me sad to think that most Americans while sitting on their blankets with their coolers beside them with their children in heated excitement scurrying around awaiting the fireworks will never give it a thought and the children will probably not be told why they are going to be seeing fireworks. Little if any thought will be given to the hundreds of thousand young Americans that have given their lives for the right they are enjoying at that very moment, while many veterans in the crowd may be reflective at moments and will be remembering and seeing the faces of friends that were absent on the their return to friendly shores.

If our Republic is to survive much longer we have to get back to the basics and reeducate our citizens as to why we are allowed to celebrate our founding and the Constitution that provided that freedom that we have cherished in the past and caused a suffering world to envy.

God Bless America!

FROM IKE'S DESK

The Crime Family! July 7, 2016

FBI Director Comey just confirmed and openly exposed the corruption of the Democrat Party and the Obama administration. Recent events have just confirmed that we have a crime family running our country; it's called the Democrat Party. The collusion between Comey, Bill Clinton, Attorney General Lynch, Hillary and President Obama could not be more apparent or different than the modus operandi of the Mafia crime family, except the Democrats are more bold and open with their objective to control all political power over the Citizens; to exercise their will as they see fit regardless of the constitution or laws. They are boldly saying loud and clear that they intend to win and don't give a damn what the responsible citizens of this country think about it because they think they have enough votes from their politically illiterates to win. Unfortunately, with the help of an impotent Republican Party; evidence appears they probably do!

The only stopping of this Democrat Crime Wave is for a mass rebellion by all segments of our society that are fed up with this political corruption and should in mass support the Republican Nominee no matter who that may be. They should be more willing to take a chance on the Pig in the Poke, than the certainty of increased slavery under the continued control of a government by the Progressive Democrats. Virtuous voting against Trump because he may not live up to your ideals of a virtuous candidate will only heighten your degradation into socialistic slavery.

The Democrat Party if they should win the upcoming election will just be emboldened to step up their cadence of march toward total social domination and the destruction of our Republic as we've known it. To once again live under Thomas Jefferson's unalienable rights may very well take generations, if at all. This could very well be the most important national election since our country's founding and may very well come down to voting for the lesser of two evils. We are being held hostage to circumstances of the times and it is of our own making. What is, Is!

Wake Up America!

If you agree, pass it on.

FROM IKE'S DESK

Republicans need a Cataclysmic Event!   July 11, 2016

Unless something cataclysmic happens against the Democrat Party momentum and in favor of the Republican Party between now and the election on November 8, The Republican Party will be no more on the morning of November 9 In politics five months is a life time and that's what it looks like it's going to take to turn events around in favor of the Republicans. They are fast running out of time and the Trump campaign will need a huge burst of support from many now unseen sources for a significant revival between now and then.

The weekly polls are out and Trump on average has made little if any gains on Hillary since he became the potential nominee. Trump's campaign has made no strives to improve those figures. His campaign struggles along with only his die hard supporters responsible for the numbers in the polls that he has had from the very beginning and many of them are now lukewarm to the repeated and worn out and recycled clichés of big beautiful walls; more jobs; greatest votes ever received; et cetera. These same worn out stump speeches are not moving new supporters to his campaign. Trump's off teleprompter speeches are not getting it done. A potential Presidential nominee needs to be able to speak in complete sentences. If he were on a high school debating team he would be losing points badly for his team.

The timing of his announcement for his Vice-Presidential running mate may very well head off any rebellion at the upcoming convention, but alone will do nothing for his standing in the November national election. As of now he and the Republican Party or losers, and if so, the saddest part is, so is our nation and so goes the future for our posterity.

How many remember the morning of November 7, 2012, when you awoke and found for certain that Obama had been reelected; that sickening and stunned realization that we were about to live under four more years of Obama and his Socialist agenda? It was extremely depressing for days afterward and those days turned out to be even worse than we had expected, but the disaster awaiting us on the morning of November 13, 2016 could be far worse and could very well shape the future direction of not only our country, but all western nations.

The Leadership of the Republican Party deserves the thrashing they may very well get this November. They have worked very hard to earn it and to some degree the average voting citizen as well for unconsciously supporting the main characters of a weak and impotent Party. However, our children and grandchildren do not! It is for them and future generations yet unborn that we must do everything possible to avoid a Democrat victory on November 9. That to-do list may have to contain a few miracles, so let's get started praying for them now.

Wake up America!

FROM IKE'S DESK

Time is running out!   **July 12, 2016**

I have voiced my opinion on several occasions concerning the negative aspects of early voting during the Primaries; however, there is another troubling practice during primary voting that is equally unfair to the citizens for their choice of party's nominee and that is States with open primaries.

Twenty-three states have open primaries, which of course mean that voters of those states may cross over and vote for a candidate in the party for which they are not registered. When you consider that Hillary from the very beginning had the Democrat Party's nomination sewed up, many democrats were free to create mischief within the republican party by crossing over and voting for what they considered the weakest republican candidate and appears many did just that and not because they all of a sudden admired the Republican candidate better. Trump won more of the open primary states and only a couple of the closed. Ted Cruz won only two open primary states, but won eight in closed primary states. This has to indicate that democrats were helping Trump in open Primary State and Cruz was receiving mostly Republican votes.

Donald Trump keeps trumpeting the fact that he has won millions of votes more than any other Republican nominee of the past. That may be true, but it's obvious that many of those votes were democrat votes? Also the Donald loves to keep telling us how many votes he received, but he doesn't keep telling us that more Republicans voted against him than for him and that's the first time that has happened for any past Republican nominee. He is the first presumptive nominee to receive a minority of votes…

When we analyze all the facts that the Republican Party is up against at this time it becomes obvious that we have a potential nominee that a very large portion of the Republican Party do not want and the majorities still should count for something, especially in politics. The question now becomes what do we do about it and when do we start? If a correction can be made it will have to be on the floor of the Republican convention with the first vote for the nominee and in order to do this the delegates must be freed to vote their conscience for the majority of republican Primary voters.

Trump has become the presumptive nominee though thoughtless voting, democrat hanky-panky, in early and open states primaries and by a minority because of an extremely large candidate field from the very beginning. Together they add up to the Republican Party stuck with a technically illegitimate and undesirable nominee and all the hell raising by his cult cannot change that fact.

Let's get real. If anything can be done it will have to start today. What are we going to do about the situation we now find ourselves? Do we do nothing and stick with Trump and work hard to try to get him elected, or do we allow the delegates to try to agree on someone else that they think will have the backing to defeat the Democrat Party in November. Yes, the choices stink, but it appears to be the only choices available.

Wake up America!

FROM IKE'S DESK

Lynch takes the Fifth! July 14, 2016

Yesterday we witnessed Loretta Lynch literally taking the Fifth Amendment in order not to incriminate herself by failing to fully answer the question put forward to her by members of the Congressional Judiciary Committee. To answer fully and honestly would have revealed her complicity and level of collusion within the Democrat Ruling Crime Family to protect Hillary Clinton from prosecution for crimes against the state.

FBI Director Comey and now the Attorney General Lynch may have just given the November election to the Republicans. Their performance during these two hearings may be the answer to a prayer by the Republicans. The level of scandal against Hillary was starting to create movement away from the Democrats to the Republicans, but now with Comey's and Lynch's conduct before the two Republican committees, they may have created the cataclysmic event I've spoken of, or at least a cause for the polls to swing away from Hillary and towards Trump.

The FBI Director and the Attorney General have proven just how bold and open the Democrat Crime Family can be to maintain power over the people. The FBI director laid out a great case for prosecution of Hillary Clinton then let her off the hook. His case against Hillary may have done the Republicans a large favor, but has personally destroyed his reputation and future credibility in the process with his final recommendation. Any serious case against Hillary's prosecution by this administration was predetermined long ago. It was obvious by Hillary's conduct throughout this period that she knew the outcome. I was right when I wrote the fix was in several months ago.

We'll have to watch the polls for the next couple of weeks to determine if there are enough honest citizens left in this country that really care. This governmental conspiracy to save Hillary, combined with Trump's pick of Vice-President and also coupled with the upcoming convention, which generally creates a slight bounce in the polls, should indicate a favorable gain by Trump. If by the beginning of the second week of August Trump is not leading Hillary in most national polling, then the chances of a Republican victory in November has not improved much and the struggle for a Republican victory will become much harder.

However I'm still hoping that the rules committee will vote to allow an open vote on the floor to release the delegates to vote their conscious. Yes, I'm still dead set against a Trump Presidency. He has said that he really is not concerned about retaining the Senate or the House. He has stated that he wants to freelance – to dictate what will or will not be; this is the mentality of a narcissistic Tyrant that should never become President of the United State of America.

Wake up America!

FROM IKE'S DESK

The Good Fight is over!   July 16, 2016

Well, the good fight is over. Those that have resisting the Trump nomination have lost the last battle before the convention begins. The Rules Committee voted last night 87-12 against freeing the delegates to vote their conscious. The Trump nomination now appears to be a certainty and the never Trump movement should now get over it and move on.

I have fought hard against this unsuited character for the Presidency from the moment he announced his candidacy in June of last year. I have fought just as hard against the Trump nomination that I did against Obama before he was elected President. I was right then and I was right to have fought just as hard against Trump becoming the Republican Nominee, but now we must move on and work toward the only future that appears available to us; the (maybe) lesser of the two evils, Trump.

Regardless of who shall win the Presidential election in November, by January 2017 the appropriate title of my next book "I told you so! Damn it!" will give me no pleasure in saying "I told you so!"

This will be the last "From Ike's Desk," until after the convention.

Wake up America!

FROM IKE'S DESK

What is truth?   **July 19, 2016**

What is truth? According to my dictionary it is reality, conformity with facts; that which accords with facts and reality. So why is it so hard for some never to be able to see truth when facts and reality is smacking them right between the eyes? Truth appears to be that which one feels comfortable with and will accept nothing short of agreement with their false beliefs. To try to reason with these misconceptions of reality are generally met with anger.

Bible verse John 8-32 tells us, "And you will know the truth, and the truth will set you free." Activists on the left have used this, except with a little twist. Gloria Steinman is credited with saying, "And you will know the truth, but first will piss you off." She appears to be far more accurate than she ever thought she would be. It appears there may very well be a much larger number of citizens that are pissed-off by the truth and do not want their comfort zone interfered with by facts that will give them the truth that counters what they have accepted that maintains their comfort.

Many may want to put the organization "Black Lives Matter" into this category, but they are wrong. Although ninety percent of the followers may not have the foggiest idea of the facts or the truth, the organization's organizers are a hate filled group that know full will their claimed cause is false, but the truth should it become known interferes with their power position to control the criminal activity for their hate filled purposes. The Truth that the police in almost every case were justified, must not be understood or believed by their followers. There is no truth in the organization, Black Lives Madder. This organization is a scourge upon our society that President Obama refuses to criticize. He legitimized their existence by inviting their leaders to the White House and If he chastised them at all, he probably ask them if they would Pretty-Please, be nice?

I believe many Trump supporters may fall into this same category. They are comfortable in their belief that Donald Trump is actually who he pretends to be and become angry when the truth becomes apparent and they will of course respond with, "Whose Truth!" Ted Cruz addressed the Texas delegation this morning. Many Trump supporters that may have watched and witnessed a politician that puts integrity and truthfulness above politics, but there engrossment with Trump runs so deep, that the truth before their eyes could not be seen, but if so, was denied because it actually makes them uncomfortable.

"To thyself, first be true," is what I have modeled my social and political life by and have always strived to look for the facts, and accept reality when it can so easily be seen. I want to know the truth even when the truth counters that which I have become comfortable in believing; to live comfortable with false assumptions serves no constructive purpose for me as a person or for society. We all must question our personal beliefs and search out the truth that validates or disputes them and be willing to accept either. "To thyself, first be true."

Note: Give serious thought to how different our country and the world would be today if Obama had been impeached and removed from office during his first term? Please give it some *serious* thought! Don't let your thoughts concerning justification distract you from the question. Think about his leadership, or the lack thereof, and the effects not only upon the citizen here at home, but also around the world.

FROM IKE'S DESK

The Presidential Campaign begins   July 22, 2016

Thanks goodness for the teleprompter. If Trump and the Republican Party want to honestly defeat Hillary this November, they must never let Trump speak off teleprompter. His handlers must keep a tight leash on him and his security must shoo away all media when he's off stage. His natural instincts will undo everything they hoped his speech was supposed to have accomplished last night.

The speech as written gave the barnyard herd enough swill to overfill the troughs many times over. The herd should have left the arena last night bloated for days to come, as well as his flock watching on television, including me. The speech writers did not miss a rock that wasn't overturned; couldn't have found another social or political problem to add. They covered every grievance that any citizen hasn't complained about since Obama started destroying our country eight years ago. Their brew had been mixed thoroughly and Trump poured it out.

Trump and the Republican Party now must stick to the script laid out last night without getting tangled up in specifics. If Trump starts freelancing and trying to explain how he can ever accomplish all that was promised last night, which of course he will not and cannot, all was for naught. Trump must maintain enough self-discipline to stay on script and continue to attack Lying Hillary.

I believe with all I've written over the past year I have proven that I'm not a fan of Donald Trump. I still believe he is possibly the worst chose of all the candidates. However, the convention has spoken and he is now the Party's nominee and unless we want another four years of Obama, we must work hard to defeat Hillary this November. This leaves us only four months to accomplish that task.

Today I start. As of this moment it is an uphill battle but besides trying to encourage enthusiasm for Trump and the Republican Party within my circle of acquaintances through direct contact, or by my emailing, I will try to find A Trump Pence Yard Sign and put it up immediately. I will try to encourage my friends and neighbors to do the same. If you don't want Hillary to win, you had better get started today as well. What will your positive actions be? What concrete effort besides saying you're for Trump will you actually do? Get over your timidity; get out and tromp the neighborhood; knock on doors and look for every opportunity you can to promote the Republican message and stress the horrors of four more years of Obama. If you don't and our efforts are all in vain, then you can kiss our country and especially the Constitution goodbye, not just for a few generations as we've been told, but forever.

Wake up America!

FROM IKE'S DESK

Party Unity   **July 23, 2016**

Party Unity? If that is really what Trump and his handlers were after, they sure made a mess of it with the Cruz speech/booing debacle. We know originally there were between five and seven hundred Cruz delegates at the convention that represented 7,637,262 of Republican voters at home; how many of them now think they have been divided from the Party by Trump's juvenile stunt of setting up delegates to Boo Cruz for not specifically coming out and saying "I support Trump," even when he knew in advance that he would not. Is this the way he plans to build unity during the campaigning between now and November?

I promised, even though I instinctively know Trump was the worse of the lot, I would support him when it became official that he was the Republican Party Nominee. I will keep that promise and do everything possible within my ability to do just that. However, will Trump start working just as hard to accomplish the same victory, or will his supporters have to go it alone? When will Trump start, or does he really intend to?

If you have been a reader From Ike's Desk, you know I've never really believed that Trump wanted to be President in the first place. His action indicate that he is more interested in feeding his insatiable ego than giving up his lavish lifestyle to live in digs below his station. I may have been wrong about this all along, but if so, when will The Donald start proving me wrong, start acting like a wannabe and commence campaigning in earnest and intelligently?

If Trump was really smart and wants to win the Presidency in November he would get off Cruz' back and stop this petty bickering. He also should show some humility and magnanimity and actually apologize to Cruz for what he said about Cruz and his family. That act alone would go a long way toward healing the divide that presently exists within the Republican Party. Cruz should then accept his apology and then we may have the workings of real unity within the Republican Party. Then, and only then, many of the eight-million Cruz voters that have decided not to vote for Trump this November will return to the flock? The numbers may be extremely large and will badly be needed if we are to win this November.

I think what we have learned during this campaign season is that that Damn Pledge has been a divider rather than a builder of unity. It has now become a political hate tool to be used to facilitate ones argument when negative emphases is needed to bolster ones point of view. It is foolhardy for any future candidate to put their name to such an agreement when the future, especially in politics is so uncertain and fluid.

Wake up America!

FROM IKE'S DESK

Something to Think About? July 26, 2016

The following was originally posted about seven weeks ago. Since then I've had two great additions suggested for Trumps Cabinet and I have now added them.

There are a few of the diehard "Never Trump" Republicans that are now returning to their roots and admitting that they will now vote for Trump. How could their choice be otherwise? The "B---h" is so corrupt that only the Devil himself could be worse, but that does not appear to be a hindrance to a large portion of our ungodly society and presently it appears there are enough of those willing to sell their souls to the devil to get her elected President.

Trump needs to trump Hillary with something other than what he has been doing or choosing a conservative Cabinet and it must be done very soon. He needs a Trump Card, and I believe his only real chance of converting many "Never Trumpers" is to pick an extremely conservative cabinet.

Many will differ with the names I have chosen for his Cabinet, but they cannot deny their history of their being conservative and the citizens would be more likely to vote for Trump knowing they have a conservative based government sitting in Washington. Cruz' name alone for the Supreme Court would stop the Supreme Court controversy in its tracks. I believe presently this is the only chance Trump has of winning the Presidency. Also those chosen have a proven ability to fight the extreme leftwing media that will counter them hard during the time remaining. A lesser known and un-tempered name will not withstand the onslaught by the radical left wing media.

Trump's Cabinet?

Secretary of Defense:	General Flynn
Attorney General:	Chris Christy
Secretary of Energy:	Sarah Palin
Secretary of Home Land Security:	Giuliani
Secretary of State:	Bolton
Appointment to Supreme Court:	Ted Cruz
Surgeon General:	Ben Carson
Secretary of Labor:	Carly Fiorina

You select the remaining positions.

Think about it? These are the most important of all cabinet position to save our Constitution and if chosen by Trump, would bring a large portion of "Never Trumpers" back to the polls, plus a large portion of un-decideds.

FROM IKE'S DESK

The corruption of our Supreme Court   August 6, 2016

On this date in 1945 80,000 people died, most were killed instantly. The B-29 bomber named the Enola Gay dropped the first atomic Weapon on the city of Hiroshima, Japan. It was the beginning of the end of the Japanese Empire and the end to World War Two. Their sacrifice possibly saved many more Japanese lives as well as maybe hundreds of thousands of American and allied forces lives as well. Less we forget…

Today, seventy-two years later we are deeply involved in another war and this one may not turn out as successful as World War Two. This may not be the death of thousands of soldiers and civilians, but could very well be the death of our nation as we've known it; and folks, that's not just hyperbole.

Sixty-two percent of our citizens oppose taxpayer funding for abortion. This shows you the power of a corrupt Supreme Court and also why you don't want Hillary as your next President.

We must remember as we go to the polls this November that the majority rules only apply as long as the Supreme Court Justices declares it so. The courts have reversed majority rights and given them to the smallest of minorities in many cases during the past eight years. They have reversed many positions held by our citizen's centuries before we became a nation.

The Supreme Court, the department of the judiciary has taken over the duties of the legislators and has made the two branches of congress irrelevant and kept the power for themselves and the executive branch – The President. This was an event the founders feared greatly as they debated the constitution. They knew that our form of government would only work as long as we elected and appointed virtuous leaders to positions of power and maintained a well civically educated society. We are now baring the consequences of the failure to heed their warning.

As I became politically conscious during my younger days, I knew long before I started studying our constitution, that the future of our entire society was held together by the flimsiest of threads vested in the flawed minds of only nine people as all minds are. These nine individuals decide what is legal and what is not. These nine have the power over the everyday lives of over three-hundred-million citizens. They have already voided the Tenth Amendment and the total destruction of our Constitution is in sight.

The lifetime appointments to the Supreme Court was thought to be a hedge against outside political influences; again considering that those appointed would be men of virtue and wiser political minds and the electorate would be wise enough to choose Presidents like minded and virtuous.

The power of these nine very human and faulted minds smacks us in the face every day and most have become so acclimated to this corruption of our constitution that they go about their daily activity accepting it as normal. The biases built into our Supreme Court by the appointment of non-virtuous and vastly more political minded individual must stop.

This is why you don't want Hillary as our next President. Will Trump's appointments be much better? The chances are that they will, but I like those chances much better than the certainty that our Bill of Rights will be as useful as an outhouse catalog under a Clinton Administration.

Wake up America!

FROM IKE'S DESK

Well! Did you all watch the Big Big Show?   August 7, 2016

I did, both of them, and they were extremely entertaining, and neither had any great surprises for me. Carly Fiorina definitely won the first as I thought she would. Greta VanSustren had a survey going during the first debate and at the end the viewers thought Fiorina won by 83%, Perry second with 7% and Jindal with 6%. That is exactly the same first three I had except I had Jindal ahead of Perry. Of course all seven were heads above the pitiful excuse for a president that now sits in the oval office.

In the prime time debate there is no doubt in my mind that Trump Trumped himself. He sat the stage at a low point by not vowing to support the winning Republican candidate and continued downward from there; he became confrontational and lambasting. He failed to answer the question directly. Overall I believe he has already seen his high point in this campaign and after last night would be surprised if by early next week he is still the front runner.

My winner of the Prime time debate was definitely Ted Cruse, Rubio and Scott Walker bringing up third place; Jeb Bush held his own; Dr. Ben Carson did himself much good and I expect to see him rise in the polls. The one hand to hand combat was between Gov. Christy and Rand Paul over violations of the Fourth Amendment of the Constitution by the government. Without going into the violations of this amendment, it is safe to say that Rand Paul was correct. Gov. Christy was unfortunately arguing from the left's socialist, feely good emotional reasoning to violate the law and Rand Paul was arguing that we are a nation of laws and must be governed by those laws. If you disagree with any amendment or law, you have the right to work to have it amended according to the Constitution, but you don't ignore it to violate it and that brings me to my next question.

Did anyone hear the word "Constitution" mentioned one time during either debate? If it was, it was in passing, but I can't remember hearing it and that is truly frightening to me. Out of all seventeen Republican candidates not to hear one candidate point out our governments total disregard for Constitutional Law is truly sad. It should have been one of the most important question ask and created the longest debate among the candidates. Our Constitution is the anchor that stabilizes our ship of state; to disregard it we become a nation adrift.

What do you think?

FROM IKE'S DESK

If you're a Conservative you must vote for trump?   August 9, 2016

How many times have you heard a pundit on television try to convince you that if you're a Conservative, you must vote for Trump? Folks that is nothing but pure Bovine Waste. To try to couple Conservatism to Trump is like trying to mix oil and water. It can't be done. Trump is not now or has never been a conservative. He is now and has always been a Democrat Liberal.

It is comical how intense Eric Bolling of Fox News can become when debating politics on television. Any negative remark against Trump by his opponent, be it Republican or Democrat, will immediately bring a scorn to Bolling's face and he will insist that if you're a conservative you have to vote for Trump. If Bolling was a true conservative himself, he would have never backed Trump in the first place. He instead would have backed a true conservative like Ted Cruz.

It was obvious there were many prominent Republican conservatives backing Trump before he became the nominee that were job hunting. There are many since he became the nominee that are now being Blackmailed into voting for Trump because he is the lesser of the two evil choices and I for one fall into that category.

I resent that fact that I must violate what I've spent a lifetime practicing because I have no other choice. Yes, I consider I've been blackmailed by a group of thoughtless primary voters caught up in Trumpmainia that numbered enough to get him nominated, even though a majority of primary voters didn't want him. In this case the system worked to the minority's advantage and to the detriment of our national health.

There are some among my readers that are dedicated and faithful

Christians and will not settle for voting for the lesser of two evils. To them, evil is evil and neither should be accepted and voted for. I can understand their position as true Christians, but I suppose I'm just not Christian enough to accept that there may be a difference of which hell on earth will be the hottest; Hillary's or Trump's? I've come to the conclusion that Hillary's hell on earth will be hotter than Trumps, so being the weak Christian that I am, I'll have to vote for Trump.

Wake up America!

FROM IKE'S DESK

Four more years of Obama?   August 15, 2016

Four more years of Obama, is that possible? Yes, according to one very possible scenario that has been forwarded. With this crazy political season anything is now possible and why not four more years of Obama? No, not Hillary, Obama!

Obama's plan goes like this. After Hillary is elected in November before she can be sworn in as President at his direction she is indicted and therefore cannot assume the Presidency. The Vice-president elect has not yet been sworn in and there is no one to fill the Presidency after January. Obama declares Marshall Law and remains the President for four more years and gets the time to finish the destruction of our country?

What? You say this is impossible? Why? There is no precedent for this and it would be difficult for the Supreme Court to rule otherwise. Ask yourself why did FBI Director Comey refuse to recommend an indictment after laying out a perfect indictment against Hillary and why did Attorney General Lynch so readily accept his recommendation not to indict when in actuality no other Attorney general would have accepted it? Isn't it possible that someone is controlling and laying a very well thought out plan to remain in office for four more years? We know Obama is not ready to give up his toy airplane and go home.

The Speaker of the house cannot assume the office of President because at the time we have a setting President and no one eligible to assume the presidency after January 20, 2017. So President Obama declares Marshall Law and issues an Executive Order citing an emergency situation and gives himself four more years in office. Keep in mind that we have a Supreme Court at the moment short one justice and the balance favors the liberal justice because of the wishy-washy history of adjudication by the supposedly conservative members. In all probability if it came to the Supreme Court, They would probably rule in Obama's favor.

Isn't conspiracy theories exciting?

Wake up America!

FROM IKE'S DESK

Seeking the Black vote!   **August 22, 2016**

If Donald trump ever expects to get a bigger percentage of the Black vote than he is already likely to get, he will have to overcome a fifty year head start by the Democrat Progressive Party; something an inapt Republican Party Leadership made no effort to do during that period and lost the Black vote forever. He will have to overcome a brainwashing and institute a reeducation program that he is not capable of, or have the time available between now and the election.

He must understand how deeply and successfully the seeds of mistrust of the Republican Party have been sewn into the brain of the

Black voter by the progressives of the Democrat Party. Trump hasn't the time for an honest reeducation of the Black voter. It will take years of presenting the truth about how and why the Democrat Party had destroyed the Black family structure and their work ethic. The Great Society and the 1964 Civil Rights Bill of President Lyndon Baines Johnson was for no other reason than to keep the N-----s down on the Democrat Plantation; reportedly his exact quote. He was a racist bigot as most elected Democrats were at that time. They still are but have changed their modus operandi and are now gathering in the Latino vote by destroying their dignity and self respect as well. Johnson had no intent of improving the Black's social standing within our society. His only goal was to insure that the Black vote stayed within the Democrat voting bloc as was the intent of all Democrat votes at that time.

Trump probably doesn't know, or if so, doesn't know how to tell Blacks that it was the Republican Party that gave them all the rights they now enjoy. From 1860s to the 1960s, over one-hundred years, the Democrat Party fought against Black Rights in every way possible. The entire south was a Black hate filled society that did everything and tried everything to keep the Blacks from voting, owning property, owning personal firearms, and living as free people. They created the Jim Crow Laws that kept Blacks at the back of the bus, different toilets and drinking fountains, from public restaurants, separate but equal education that was not equal and was actually substandard, voting against all anti-lynching laws and it was so easy for the Democrats. They created the cast system of elevating the lowest white person above all blacks no matter how successful the black may be. The poor white trash was lord over all blacks and considered superior and they voted to constantly suppress Blacks from climbing to their level.

Can Trump convince the Black voters that it was the Democrats Party that voted against all their rights and make them believe it? Can he tell them and make them believe that most of their civil rights law was passed with only a few and sometimes not a single Democrat Senator's vote? Can he make them believe that the Thirteenth, Fourteenth, and Fifteenth Amendments that gave them the same equal rights as all citizens were all passed by a majority of Republican votes? Can he convince them that the Democrat Party today only exists by depriving the Blacks of their dignity and work ethic by a system of redistribution of wealth? No he cannot!

If he tells the truth he will be crucified by the left wing media and Hillary. They will turn it all around and make him look like a clown and he will become a racist. The Black vote can only change through a slow and awakening of the true intent of the Democrat Party by the Blacks themselves. They will have to reclaim their own dignity and self respect and I doubt Trump can show them the way. At this stage of the campaign any attempt will meet with meager success and could seriously backfire.

Wake up America!

FROM IKE'S DESK

The Republican Primary System must Change   August 27, 2016

The problems encountered with selecting the Republican Nominee this year could not have been more obvious to the Republican voter. The Republican voter must demand changes that are not only fair to the voter but also the various candidates. There are, in my opinion, several things that would be a major improvement over what has occurred in the past.

First, I would prefer that early voting be eliminated, however if necessary at least the time cut by half. It is unfair to all concerned when there is so much information that comes to light concerning various candidates after the first early votes have been cast. It's unfair because the voter can't change their mind and also it's unfair to the other candidates they may have received that vote instead.

Second, the primary voting season by the various states need to be reduced to about three months or less. The states could be broken down into three groups and hold a Super Tuesdays thirty days apart. This would mean the primary voting would be over within two months and the nominee chosen. Currently the first State Primary is held on February 1st and the last on June 7. This drags out the process to over five months. This serves mostly the industries of the Media, advertizing and political pundits and is overall detrimental and extremely costly to the candidates and the voters become tired and lose interest.

Third, the different methods of voting by states for candidates need not change, but I personally prefer the Caucus method best. It's a system that makes the voters become involved and if you don't want to become involved you probably shouldn't be voting anyway.

Fourth, I would recommend that all states have the same guidelines for their delegates. One state should not have a rule that their delegates must vote three times for their candidate before being free to vote their conscious and another state's delegates only one. There should be uniformity within the rules. I would prefer one time only then open up the convention. If there is that much dissention within the delegation at the convention that they are demanding a floor vote to open the convention, then there is something wrong with the Nominee, and the open convention sounds like a wise decision. As evidenced by this year's outcome.

Fifth, no open Republican Primary Voting. No one votes in the Republican Primary except registered Republicans. We must not let the opposition interfere with the integrity of our voting process as has happened this year.

We now know that the GOP really screwed up this convention, by manipulated the floor vote to prevent the delegates from voting on an open convention. I and many have come to the conclusion now that the GOP would rather lose an election than relinquish their power over the convention.

We have four years to think about much that has happened during this past election and maybe a lifetime of regrets, but will necessary changes ever take place as long as the same Republican Leadership remains? Conservatives Republicans must take back their party or there will be no Republican Party for the election of 2020!

Wake up Republican Voters.

FROM IKE'S DESK

The Media Show will Begin   **September 26, 2016**

The Media show, maybe better known as the "Debate" is about to begin and that is really what it's all about – The Media! There will not be a network that will not be covering the event all day long. They will generate billions of dollars in commercial time on their airways. They will generate hype to increase the coverage so they can charge more for commercial time building up to the debate and the results when all is said and done from these phony debates could and will damaged our country tremendously far reaching into the future.

Here, I'm speaking to the educated voter. You know who you are! You also know at this moment who you will be voting for and tomorrow morning after all is said and done, your vote will not have changed because of this phony dog and pony show that has been hyped by the media. You know who is running; Hillary and Trump, and by now know the records of them both and there Party over the years and just because there is a gaffe; a flub; or whatever by the one you will be voting for during the debate, will not change your vote on November 8th, Right? So, nothing really was accomplished for you except for maybe another way to waste a perfectly good evening that could have best been spent watching old Roy Roger Movies.

I have been watching these debates since Nixon and Kennedy and not once during all those debates has the Party I intended to vote for changed. Came the November General election and I voted for the Party and their candidate that I knew would better serve our country. Just because Nixon had perspiration on his upper lip and Kennedy appeared calm and cool, Shouldn't have changed ones opinion about what political philosophy would better serve our country; but it did and in a big way.

The debates during every election cycle since that first with Nixon and Kennedy has elected the candidate that had the fewest flaws, gaffes, and mistakes and to hell with political philosophy. We no longer give a damn about what is right for the country, only who looked and debated the best. What a hell of a way to pick a President. The direction our country has taken toward socialism is proof positive that the good citizen of this country has now and probably forever accepted as President who the Media declares the winner.

This morning I will hear from all the expert political pundants who won the debate and therefore who will be our next President. Again – What a hell of a way to choose a President!

Did I watch this debate – NO! I made better use of my time by writing letters to family members. I've always known who I'm going to vote for.

FROM IKE'S DESK

"IF" October 18, 2016

"IF" is such a small word, but large enough to change the world, *If* only a certain event would have turned out differently. *If only* Donald Trump had not felt he was qualified to be President what would the polls show today? *If only* so many had not bought into his demagogic rhetoric we would have a nominee running many points ahead of Hillary today. *If only* the news media had not convinced the masses that the way to elect a President is by debates, they may still be voting with their brains. We can debate for years to come who is to blame for losing our country, *If only*.

I could drag this post out forever, *If only* there was a need. The people may win yet, but, *If only* God will help us.

FROM IKE'S DESK

The Christian majority – Where were you? October 27, 2016

Where has the Christian majority been during the last few decades as the secular forces went to war against Christianity within our country and around the world? Was "Onward Christian soldiers, marching as to war," just hollow words in old scrubby Church Song Books that many voices sung with enthusiasm and vigor throughout the churches of America for years, but evidently held no real understanding that there would be a day that they would indeed need to fight that war in order to maintain their Christian faith? Had it been so, Christianity would not be the only religion that can be publically scorned and ridiculed today without serious repercussions.

Where was this so-called Christian army that should have been fighting against the takeover of the Republican Party by a secular enemy during the Primary voting period? Why did this Christian Army not stand up and fight for the Christian values their voices were so proudly and loudly proclaiming throughout sanctuaries across our vast land? Why were their song of praise and thankfulness for his power and assurance so important inside the sanctuaries but held no consequences at the Ballot Box? Why did so many not practice in society that the proclaimed in church? Had they truly understood what happens outside of their sanctuaries will eventually effect what can happen to their Christian Church inside and out, their casting of votes may very well have nominated a Christian during the Republican Party presidential campaign instead of a secular Charlatan. Had they practiced outside what they preached inside, we very well could have had a Christian family living in the White House in January.

The massive numbers of Christians throughout our land were sufficient enough to have elected a Republican nominee that could truly have made America Great Again, but failed to vote their Christian values. What were you so-called Christians thinking? Or better still, why weren't you thinking? Now you'll have to settle for worse or worser!

FROM IKE'S DESK

The Final November 8, 2016

Today, the most perfect political system ever devised in the history of mankind may very well be destroyed and probably never to be lived again in many generation regardless of who gets elected. However, the only chance for the possibility to remain as free as we are today and for our posterity is with a vote for Donald Trump. A win for Hillary will mean the paper our Constitution is written on holds no more usefulness to our citizens than toilet tissue.

After fighting the Socialist Democrat Party for the last fifty-six years, there would be only one choice left for me. I made up my mind long ago that I would vote for Ted Cruz and not Trump if it looked like Trump had it sewn up and wouldn't need my vote, or I would vote for Ted Cruz if Trump was so far behind that my vote would do him little good; either way I was off the hook and wouldn't have to vote for Trump and against everything I've stood for and fought for my entire political life. Now that the statistics indicate that the election could go either way I find myself in the situation I've always hoped I could avoid. Today will also be the start of my final book, "Well, I told you so! Damn it!"

It has been no secret that I believe Donald Trump has been the most unsuited nominee the Republican Party could have possibly chosen from the original seventeen that threw their hats in the ring. The reason we had so many Republican candidates was because the pickin's looked so easy. Obama and the Democrat party had created so much dissatisfaction within the electorate that all thought the people would consider them a better Presidential choice than anything the Democrats could throw against them; and of course they would have. Any one of the sixteen except Trump would be many points ahead of Hillary Clinton at this very moment if the egotistical Demagogue, who was never a Republican, had not jumped in and spoiled it for the citizens and the Republican Party.

Ever since Trump has secured the nomination he has demonstrated his inability to control his juvenile and gargantuan egotistical impulses to spitefully crucify anyone that may disagree or use disparaging remakes against him which is the signature of a mental midget; not the maturity and mentality needed to serve as our President. His momentary pretentions of being Presidential will no longer exist if he should win the White House; he will immediately resort to his juvenile temperament the moment the election has been won.

I fought hard against Trump becoming the Republican nominee from the very beginning. I knew when he declared his candidacy that he was mentally unsuited to sit in the Oval Office. I knew he was just as unsuited for the office of President as I predicted Obama was before he was elected. I was as right about Obama as I am about Trump.

This may well be the last of the Fourteen Presidential elections the good Load has allowed me the right to exercise my civic duty. Considering my political philosophy for the past fifty-six years, to vote against everything I have fought for would be a vote for either Trump or Hillary and today I find that by voting for Trump I am violating that principal I have lived by my entire life. It makes me sick to my stomach to think that the choice of worse and worser are the only two available when we could have had a real honest Christian nominee that loves his country and understands the Constitution and what our founding fathers really stood for and sacrificed their fortunes and lives for if only Christian and conservative voters had voted with their hearts and minds instead of being sucked into following this Pied Piper. In January we could have had a real Christian family sitting in the White House that would have restored honesty, decency and respect to our government once more. Now, we are going to have a complete socialist or a Pig-in-the-Poke.

From the very beginning I was for Ted Cruz and he almost made it, but unfortunately a minority of politically thoughtless minds captured by a true demagogue had other ideas and they got what they wished for; a nominee totally unsuited to be President. A nominee the majority of Primary Republican voters voted against.

I also said at the time that if Trump became the Republican Nominee I would work just as hard for him against the Democrat candidate as I would have for Ted Cruz had he become the nominee. When I said that I knew to defend and support Trump would take more forced enthusiasm and phony-ism than I was possibly capable of, but I thought it would be necessary to prevent a Democrat from winning and at least I would try. Let happen what happens and I'll have to learn to live with violating everything I've stood for my entire political life – "First to thyself be true!"

At age 87 and after fighting against the Democrat Socialist Party for all my adult life, I now find the energy and enthusiasm that was once the driving force that kept me fighting against their evils that was diluting the purposes of our Democratic Republic and kept me going is fast waning. Father Time is starting to win out over body and mind and is telling me it's time to give up and turn the fight over to others that still believe our country as envisioned by our founders is still worth fighting for. However, if there is any fight left in anyone against our nation's Slouching Toward Gomorra, it will have to be they that continue the fight, because today I will be forced to violate my principals and vote druthers instead of for a true American that could have really made our country great again.

Today I am alone. The true purpose; the reason and the guiding light that has made my life worth living these past sixty-three years is no longer beside me and life has lost its enthusiasm and drive so therefore today's, From Ike's desk, will be my last. For those of you that have just let out a big shout of Halleluiah, thanks for hanging in there as long as you did. For those that have read my posts over the years and given me the feedback that encouraged me to continue the fight, I truly thank you. This post is the last publically political statement I ever intend to make, except for my final book "Well, I told you so, Damn It!"

If Hillary should win today, and it looks like she probably will, I have to say with heavy heart that there will be many sick and disillusioned Trump supporters and all I ask of them is do not put that big "IF" blame on everyone else that said they would not support him and didn't from the very beginning; they are not the ones Responsible for the lost liberties are citizens will be experiencing almost immediately.

God bless you all and let's hope that God comes back and blesses America again because he has either left us or you *so-called* Christians have betrayed him – you decide how you're going to alibi your way out of this if Trump loses?

Gene Nelson Isom

Epilogue

That Final From Ike's Desk was written November the 8th, the morning of the election. I retired for the night early and was sickened by the knowledge that Hillary was to be our next President and resigned to the fact that we were going to face eight more years of the Obama administration. I knew that by the next morning our country as we have known it was over. I knew I had fought the good fight the best that I knew how, but had lost. I had that same nauseous and disgusted feeling that had hindered sleep the nights of the two previous Presidential Elections with the defeat of McCain and Romney, but there was still hope; not this time. I had resigned myself to the fact that with what time I had left on earth it would be a gradual turn toward servitude under a Socialist Administrations.

When I arose the morning of November the 9th, I was in no particular hurry to hear the sickening jubilation coming from the most corrupt individual that ever had the nerve to run for President of the United States of America, Hillary Clinton. I leisurely made my coffee and went through my normal morning routine, using as much time as I could to avoid the eventual need to turn on the television.

When the tube lit up there sat my morning friends from FOX News. Their jovial manner was puzzling but soon understandable when

I learned that Donald Trump was now the President of the United States. I sat numb for a moment before jumping straight up spilling my coffee in the most vulnerable spot causing my yelps to be much louder than originally intended. The jubilation I felt at that moment soothed any discomfort I was feeling from hot spilled coffee. And as they say, the rest is history. Well, not quite yet!

Today is March 3, 2017 and Donald Trump was sworn in as our President on January 20, 2017, and of this writing has been in office only forty-one days and the corrupt, evil and anti-American Democrat Socialist Party and their brain-dead membership have already perched and have been pecking at his bones as I predicted they would. He has however demonstrated that he does have the stamina and fortitude to withstand their dishonest and hateful onslaught to this point and may make a Great President if he can muster the help and unity of our failed Republican leadership. Trumps biggest obstacle to accomplishing all he promised may not be the radical left leaning media and their dominion after all, but may very well be prominent members of his own party that have never been bashful about showing their contempt for Trump. If Trump can unify the Republican Party behind him there will be nothing that he and they cannot accomplish within a relatively short time.

The hand holding back the throttle of the engine of progress within our society for too long has belonged to the radical liberal left and especially these last eight years under an American hating excuse for a President named Barrack Huiesian Obama. He kept the throttle in idle as the Chinese, India and much of the middle East push their throttles wide open. Consider what we were capable of accomplishing in the past within a relatively short time; the Alaska Highway and hundreds of thousands of aircraft, tanks, weapons of all descriptions within one year. I read where it took New York City billions of dollars and ten years just to build a subway that ran only twenty blocks. Trump could possible accomplish almost everything he promised within the first four years of his Presidency If he could but only muster the unity and the will of the people. I'm convinced we Americans can accomplish anything we choose to if we could only agree to come together and get it done.

No, the history of the Trump Presidency is yet to be written. I can imagine with a bit of certainty that there will be many moments of jubilation and disappointment by his supporters over the coming year. I don't know how all my predictions of Trumps administration that were made during the 2016 election campaigning will turn out. I know in normal times he was definitely not the man for the job, but considering the times, condition and direction this country was heading, he may turn out being the man needed at this moment in time. However, I'm still a little skeptical.

I've said to many of my friends that I cannot complete this book until July of 2017 when I could then predict with some certainty the outcome of the Trump Presidency. My predictions over the years to gain control of over fifty percent of the electorate will be intensified against Trump's Administration. My knowledge and fight against some within the Republican Party leadership over the years convinces me that many will join forces with the left and fight against Trump just as hard. With only 60 days into his Presidency much of this is now happening.

Many on the left are now predicting that he will not last his first term, but will resign because of his inability to keep his promises. I can easily visualize that happening because of my feeling, and I've expressed it many times during the campaign period of 2016, that this was an ego trip for Trump from the very beginning. If that should happen it is over; Trump will turn out to be the Pied-Piper that killed America. On the other hand if he is truly the individual he has convinced his followers he is and has the strength and support he needs to accomplish his promises to the American people, he could very well save America and be the greatest of all past Presidents.

It is now mid July 2017 and I can now bring this book to a close with my predictions of what was to come is now in the making. Trump is up against what no President before him has had to endure; a hate filled Democrat Party that will not accept the will of the people and a Republican Leadership that has reneged on their promises to the citizens that elected them and in direct opposition to all that Trump had promised and was elected. Our country has survived these two-hundred plus years only because the losing party has accepted the results of the elections.

Up and until the day of the election I was convinced that Trump was the wrong man for the job of President of the United States of America, and still believe under normal times that would have been so; however, I am now convinced that only Trump among the seventeen Republican candidates that started the run for the nomination of the Republican Party could have beaten Hillary Clinton.

The outcome of the Trump administration is yet to be written. The struggle will be long and hard and will only succeed if Trump can get the leadership of the Republican Party to fulfill their promises to the citizens that voted for them. Only then will Trump and America win.

THE END

www.ingramcontent.com/pod-product-compliance
Lightning Source LLC
Chambersburg PA
CBHW020052170426
43199CB00009B/262